D1233385

THE YORKHILL STORY

The History of
The Royal Hospital for Sick Children
Glasgow

THE YORKHILL STORY

❋

The History of
The Royal Hospital
for
Sick Children
Glasgow

by

EDNA ROBERTSON

Printed in Great Britain by
Robert MacLehose and Company Limited
The University Press, Glasgow
for
The Board of Management for Yorkhill
and Associated Hospitals, Glasgow
1972

Foreword

In 1964, during the celebration of the fiftieth anniversary of the opening of the Royal Hospital for Sick Children at Yorkhill, it was suggested to the Board of Management that a history of the hospital might be written. At the time nothing tangible resulted. Later when, as this history relates, structural faults in the old hospital were discovered, and it was decided that the old building must be demolished and a new hospital built on the same site, the Board realised that if a history were not written immediately not only would much interesting material be lost but, worse still, many of the contacts with former members of the staff would vanish. This was unthinkable, and in 1969 the decision to proceed with the writing of this history was made.

Once the decision had been taken it became evident that the main problem was not the availability of material but to find the right person with the inclination and time to do the necessary research and with the ability to write a living story setting the Royal Hospital for Sick Children in its context in the history of Glasgow. In the event it was a mixture of discreet enquiry and good luck that brought together the Board and Miss Edna Robertson, the author of this history. Miss Robertson is assistant features editor on the staff of the *Glasgow Herald* and she has a particular interest in the sociological background of Glasgow. The history of the hospital which she has written has blended the formal story recorded in the minute books and records, the social story as it appears in the files of the *Glasgow Herald* and elsewhere, and the human side as told by former members of the staff. The Board place on record their profound thanks to Miss Robertson for writing a history which, starting with the upsurge of interest in child health in the latter half of the last century, recounts the enthusiasm, determination, and energy which gave birth to what is now Scotland's largest children's hospital and tells how the cherished reputation of that hospital has been won.

The whole costs of the publication of this history are being generously donated by four friends of the hospital, each of whom has been associated with and has taken a close interest in the hospital over the past 50 years. To these friends, whose request for anonymity must be respected, the Board extend their grateful thanks.

Since the printing of this history has been completed the Board have learned with the greatest of pleasure that the hospital is to be honoured by an inaugural visit from Her Majesty the Queen on 6th July 1972.

RICHARD H. BARCLAY
Chairman

Board of Management for Yorkhill
and Associated Hospitals

Glasgow, April 1972

Contents

Foreword   *page* 5
Acknowledgements   8

  1   THE CHILDREN OF THE POOR   9
  2   BATTLE ROYAL   17
  3   CROSSES AND VEXATIONS   20
  4   GARNETHILL   28
  5   THE FIRST DOCTORS   34
  6   UNFUSSY PHILANTHROPY   42
  7   VICTORIAN FUND-RAISING   46
  8   THE DISPENSARY   52
  9   TOWN AND COUNTRY   65
 10 NEW CHIEFS   74
 11 THE GREEN SLOPES OF YORKHILL   80
 12 A STATE OCCASION   91
 13 MILITARY OCCUPATION   95
 14 YORKHILL AND GILMOREHILL   99
 15 PAEDIATRIC PIONEERING   110
 16 VIEW FROM THE BOARDROOM   123
 17 SOMETHING TO CELEBRATE   130
 18 CHILDREN IN WARTIME   144
 19 NATIONAL HEALTH   148
 20 PAEDIATRICIANS' PROGRESS   154
 21 RESEARCH   167
 22 NURSING   173
 23 THE GREAT MIGRATION   181
 24 YORKHILL REGAINED   187

Appendix: Consultants at the Royal Hospital for Sick
  Children at the time of the move back to
  Yorkhill from Oakbank, 15th October 1971   195
Bibliography   196
Index   198

Acknowledgements

THE hospital's formal records, dating from the first entry in the promoters' minute book in 1861, have provided the necessary framework for this history. I am grateful to Mr Richard H. Barclay and his colleagues on the board of management for allowing me access to these records, and for advice and co-operation.

Many people have generously provided information and lent books, journals, and photographs. Among former members of the hospital staff I should like especially to thank Professor Stanley Graham, Mr James Methven, Miss M. O. Robinson, Miss Ruth Clarkson, Mr Andrew P. Laird, Dr Agnes Cameron, and Dr Mary Stevenson. Many members of the present-day staff have provided much valuable information. I should like in particular to thank Mr Stewart Mann, whose knowledge of the hospital's history was of immeasurable help; Professor James H. Hutchison and Professor Gavin C. Arneil, for their painstaking assistance in the sections of this book dealing with medical and research developments; Mr Wallace Dennison, who provided similar information on the surgical side; Miss Olive Hulme, who supplied valuable information on nursing; and, on the administrative side, Dr Hugh Park, and Mr Robert Dunlop and members of his staff at the group's West Regent Street offices.

My thanks are due also to Dr A. K. Bowman; to Mr Alfred Lochhead; to Dr J. M. A. Lenihan, of the Western Regional Hospital Board; to Sister Mary Camillus, of the staff of Garnethill Convent School; to Miss Elizabeth Wilson, of the library of the Royal College of Physicians and Surgeons of Glasgow; and to the staff of the *Glasgow Herald* library.

Finally, I should like to acknowledge the help given in the production of this book by Mr J. B. Fleming, who designed the jacket; by Mr William Bryson, of Robert MacLehose and Company Limited; by Mr Joseph Devlin, the hospital's medical illustrator, who took most of the photographs illustrating the recent history of Yorkhill; and by Mrs Margaret Swift, who typed the manuscript.

E.R.

ILLUSTRATIONS

Most of the illustrations of the hospital, past and present, are from the collection of Yorkhill and Associated Hospitals. The photographs on pages 92, 103 (lower), 183, and 190 are reproduced by kind permission of the *Glasgow Herald*.

Chapter I

THE CHILDREN OF THE POOR

'OUR proceedings here this day,' announced Archibald Orr Ewing, M.P., 'will put an end to a sort of disgrace which has been attached to the city of Glasgow in not having had a children's hospital amidst this vast population.'

Orr Ewing was presiding over the official opening of the Glasgow Hospital for Sick Children, and it was not surprising that his speech was sharply worded. The 'disgrace' of which he spoke had not been easily remedied; launching a children's hospital in Victorian Glasgow – where more than half the annual deaths were of children under the age of five – had proved no simple matter. Not everyone had rallied to the cause, and the idea had been talked about, fought for, and argued over for more than 20 years before that opening ceremony late in 1882. 'The Sick Kids', as the hospital has been affectionately known for decades, has a long and stormy prehistory and one that touches the life of the city at many points.

It all began on a January afternoon in 1861. A 'meeting of gentlemen' had been summoned by circular in the Religious Institution Rooms at the corner of Buchanan Street and Dundas Street. Leading medical men, leading clergymen, and assorted other influential citizens attended. Unanimously they resolved that the infant mortality rate in Glasgow 'loudly calls for the adoption of preventive measures', and, further, that the best possible preventive measure was the establishment of a children's hospital. They then set about electing a committee to collect subscriptions and to look out for a suitable site.

The proposal which was given its first formal expression on that occasion appears to have been originally mooted by two medical men – Dr John B. Cowan, who was one of the conveners of that inaugural meeting, and Dr George H. B. Macleod, who was also present. Both men were then in their thirties; both had served as doctors in the Crimea; and both, since their return to Glasgow, were embarking on eminent careers. Macleod was later to succeed Lister in the Chair of Surgery at Glasgow University; Cowan was to become Professor of Materia Medica.

Macleod was a tall, strikingly handsome man, always immaculately clad in morning coat and well-pressed trousers. 'Good looks are always an advantage to medical men,' slyly noted a journalist of the time. 'Dr George is handsome, and knows it.' Later, because of his stately and deliberate manner, he was to be nicknamed 'the Duke' by generations of students at Glasgow University; and after receiving his knighthood he was known on occasion to reprimand those who addressed him as 'Dr' instead of 'Sir'. He himself always scrupulously observed the courteous formalities, doffing his hat to students in the street. 'I long ago made up my mind that if I could teach the student nothing else, I could teach him manners,' he remarked.

Though he was one of the first to accept the teachings of Lister, Macleod himself was a good, capable, practical surgeon rather than a pioneer. Warm-hearted and considerate beneath his stateliness, he was credited with 'the great merit of always looking at a case rather from the patient's point of view than from the strictly surgical'. The movement for a children's hospital was not his first foray into philanthropy; a few years earlier he had advocated the establishment on the Clyde coast of sanatoria for the poor and their children.

Macleod came of a Highland family which was (and still is) distinguished in the pulpit rather than the operating theatre – his brother was the renowned Dr Norman Macleod, minister of the Barony Church. John B. Cowan, on the other hand, belonged to a family which had practised medicine in and around Glasgow since the early seventeenth century.

Cowan had studied in Germany, Paris, Edinburgh, and Dublin as well as in Glasgow. Once launched on his career, he played an active part in medical reform and was closely associated with the transfer of the Glasgow medical school from the Royal Infirmary to the Western. He was also for a time editor of *The Glasgow Medical Journal*. The logical precision of his thought, and his impressive powers of generalisation and classification, won him much praise. He was, as one of his colleagues put it, 'well able to seize the opportunities for advancement as they came his way.' Like Macleod, who was an honorary vice-president of the children's hospital for many years, Cowan maintained his early association with the movement and was chairman of the committee of management responsible for the hospital when it opened.

George Macleod. This drawing appeared in the Glasgow 'Bailie'.

But if Macleod and Cowan could in some degree claim credit for originally advancing the idea – and Macleod was later to refer to the 'scheme which, along with Professor Cowan, I suggested more than 30 years ago' – many others must have been simultaneously coming round to the same way of thinking. The need was obvious; the precedents were plentiful. From Copenhagen to Constantinople, from St Petersburg to Boston, a rash of children's hospitals had spread during the 1830s, '40s, and '50s. Paris had had one since the beginning of the century. In London, where there had been a children's dispensary since 1769, a children's hospital was opened at Great Ormond Street in 1852; and London was soon followed by Liverpool, Manchester, and, in 1860, by Edinburgh (a consideration which cannot have been absent from the minds of those who attended the inaugural meeting in the Religious Institution Rooms). Glasgow in 1861 was one of the few major cities in Europe still without a children's hospital; and at no time and in no place could the need have been greater.

★   ★   ★

The city was growing and prospering in that year of the inaugural meeting. The 1850s had brought more power looms and more spindles as well as, in rich abundance, more people. Despite the financial panic of 1857 it had been, by and large, a decade of progress. Business and the manufacturing trades were booming; the first iron ships were being built on the Clyde; and though in that January of 1861 the news from across the Atlantic was ominous, the American Civil War with its dire effects on the cotton trade was still in the future. Glasgow was flourishing, and many Glaswegians were flourishing with her.

Thousands of others were not. It was a desperately far cry from the handsome terraces of the west-end to the shabby single-ends of Cowcaddens or the shoddily built 'back-lands' round Glasgow Cross.

The city had grown too rapidly in the Industrial Revolution. In 1791 Glasgow, still considerably smaller than Edinburgh, had a mere 66,000 inhabitants. By 1831 there were more than 200,000. Thousands more flooded in during the 'hungry forties'; in the '50s the population increased by 20 per cent; and in that year of 1861 it was pushing 400,000 – more if you counted the suburbs. Glasgow in that year was more densely populated than any other city in the kingdom except Liverpool, and in places the density was almost 200 persons per acre.

If many of the Highland and Irish newcomers were ill-equipped to cope with city life, the city was in even greater measure ill-equipped to cope with its new citizens. There was no tradition of city planning on which to draw, nor was there, in that age of *laissez faire*, any great will to plan. Growth was too often haphazard.

Two decades earlier Edwin Chadwick, Commissioner of the Poor Laws, had recorded a sharp criticism of Glasgow both for its structural arrangements and the condition of its population. Chadwick said he had never seen misery equal to Glasgow's in any other British city (next in line was Edinburgh). Had he returned to Glasgow in 1861 he would hardly have wished to eat his words. There had of course been improvements. Loch Katrine water, for example, was introduced in 1857 – but only for those with 5s to spare for a key to one of the city taps; many still drew water from the wells. The Public Health (Scotland) Act was not passed until 1867; public health reform was slower in Scotland than in England, though the need was even greater. The eighteenth century had seen an encouraging growth of civic responsibility in such matters, with a promising start to the hospital and dispensary movement, but the spirit flagged badly amid the complexities of Victorian society and the individualistic trend of Victorian thought. The great period of Glasgow's sanitary reform, and with it the education of public opinion, did not get properly under way until the last third of the century. Glasgow in 1861 still had no medical officer of health, no municipal sanitary department, no fever hospital.

Living conditions were vile in the wynds and vennels of the city. As Glasgow's first medical officer of health was to put it some years later:— 'There is not merely overcrowding of the ground space with houses and with tenements, but there is overcrowding of the tenements with rooms, and of the rooms with persons.' In 1861 a quarter of the city's population lived in single-ends, and 22,000 of these single-ends housed seven or more people. In Glasgow in the 1860s, and for many years to come, there were people living in windowless cellars; in hovels with earthen floors; in tenements where human excrement was disposed of through the windows; in dwellings where the infirmary van had been known to call six times in one day.

Ventilation was abysmal. The son of a Victorian general practitioner once wrote that 'part of my father's armamentarium was a good thick stick. This was not a weapon either of defence or offence: he used it for the purpose of breaking windows and letting in air.' If the windows were merely opened, they would be slammed shut again immediately the doctor left.

Festering rubbish heaps, faulty drains, and polluted water made the city a prey to recurrent epidemics from 1816 onwards. Tales told by the survivors of some of the cholera epidemics horribly resembled Defoe's descriptions of the Great Plague. Dead-carts rumbled through the city streets at night, and victims were buried in common pits which were kept open till the correct quota of bodies had arrived. And Glasgow in 1861, though it had seen the worst of the epidemics, had not yet seen the last.

13

Even in non-epidemic years, the death toll was sometimes between 30,000 and 40,000. Infectious diseases spread rapidly in overcrowded slums lacking sewers and drains; tuberculosis caused many deaths. Poverty, overwork, and undernourishment were prevalent. Besides the chronic poor there were many who were brought near to destitution by unemployment in a slump period – and Poor Relief was more stringently administered in Calvinistic Scotland than in England. A diet overloaded with porridge and potatoes resulted in deficiency diseases. Crippling bone diseases and disfiguring skin diseases were commonplace in the slums. One index of the general ill-health was that the minimum height for recruitment to the Army had to be lowered four inches in a lifetime.

The children of the poor suffered grievously. In the very week that the hospital promoters held their preliminary meeting the city chamberlain issued his statistics for the previous year. These showed a general death rate of 1 to 33 of the population, and 'upwards of half' the deaths were of children under five.

A year earlier an eminent Glasgow doctor had listed in order of importance the five main causes of infantile deaths:— overcrowding and vitiated air, together with poor drainage and inadequate light; deficient nutrition; 'want of a hospital for sick children'; early marriages; and neglect of illegitimate children.

The children of the poor were born in filthy dwellings; the birth was often complicated by pelvic deformities caused by rickets; mothers were frequently drunk during the delivery, and many hurried back to work as soon as they were able to struggle out.

For the survivors the prospects were often bleak. The insurance of children against death was believed to lead to many murders. Baby farming – the boarding out of children with an old woman who might take in any number at a time – was common practice, and often no questions were asked if the child died. Many of the children thus disposed of were illegitimate. Social welfare was concerned with the administration of the Poor Law rather than with public health, and illegitimacy tended to be viewed more in terms of the cost of pauperism than of the wellbeing of the child.

Bow-legged from rickets, the children of the slums were also a prey to nervous diseases, convulsions, hydrocephalus, tubercular diseases, scarlet fever (often extremely virulent), mumps, and smallpox – and to sheer neglect and debility. Many died of diseases that have long since ceased to be considered deadly; and many died without having seen a doctor. It was well known, pointed out Dr John B. Cowan, addressing the inaugural meeting in 1861, that many children of the poor in Glasgow received no medical attention except when it was too late to be of any avail.

The feeling still lingered, and not only among the poor, that it was better to entrust a sick infant to a neighbouring 'auld wife' than to a doctor. Another popular alternative to the doctor was the druggist. One Glasgow physician wrote despairingly of 'those who are tempted to trust blindly to penny powders obtained at random from the chemist's shop and the soothing syrups advertised in the windows.' Opium was the main ingredient in some of these drugs.

Even when a doctor was called in, his healing powers were likely to be limited by lack of knowledge – children's diseases were still generally treated as a branch of obstetrics, and medically the child tended to be regarded as a miniature adult. Many serious ailments were dismissed as teething trouble. This in itself was a powerful argument for the establishment of a children's hospital, where knowledge of the diseases of childhood could be fostered. Another argument was that parents who dreaded the idea of taking a child to the infirmary might feel differently about a hospital exclusively for children.

★   ★   ★

It was against this depressing background that the hospital promoters held their inaugural meeting. But if the movement was begun not a day too early in terms of public need, it was a few years too early for public opinion. William T. Gairdner knew what he was up against when he became Glasgow's first medical officer of health in 1863. He spoke of 'the fear and the certainty, indeed, that we could not propose, with any chance of carrying public opinion with us, measures of the extremely strong and radical order that are absolutely necessary to cope with the immense evils we have to deal with.' There were even protests when Gairdner, with reason to fear an outbreak of cholera, closed all the remaining private wells in the city. Afterwards a member of Glasgow Corporation, carping about the cost of the operation, concluded his peroration by remarking, 'And the cholera never came.' This may have been an extreme example, but public opinion in Glasgow certainly contrasted with that of radical Birmingham, where the promoters of a children's hospital also held their inaugural meeting in 1861 – and the first patients were admitted within a year. Glasgow's first patients were admitted 22 years after the inaugural meeting.

Many individuals, it is true, dedicated themselves to the destitute. Chadwick's revelations of working-class conditions had touched many consciences – and so, too, at about the same time, had Dickens's tale of Tiny Tim with his little crutch and his 'limbs supported by an iron frame.' Institutions like the Merchants' House and the Trades House had long concerned themselves with the relief of poverty, and for decades members of the medical profession had campaigned against the prevailing conditions. But around them was an ocean of apathy and ignorance. The year of the inaugural meeting, 1861, was also the year when the capsizing of the Govan ferry, with the loss of seven lives, cast a gloom over the city. But not everyone who mourned the sad loss of those seven lives was conscious of the everyday tragedies of the slums. 'Many were not aware of what others lacked, in the Cowcaddens or the Grassmarket,' as the historian Agnes Mure Mackenzie put it.

As well as ignorance there was fatalism, in that age of large families, towards the death of infants and children. And in an era of rampant individualism the notion was dying hard that disease afflicted the poor because they were intrinsically inferior. In the public mind social evils were not yet clearly related to public health; not everyone realised that frequently the poor were ill precisely because they were poor. Moreover if Glasgow medical opinion was clearer on these matters it was still, for other reasons, divided about the desirability of separate hospitals for children; and when the promoters of the hospital ran into opposition from the medical Establishment, as they very quickly did, public opinion was not strong enough to carry them through the crisis.

Chapter 2

BATTLE ROYAL

EVEN at that first meeting in January 1861, there had been behind
the formal unanimity a strong hint of opposition. Among the speakers
was David Smith, a director of Glasgow Royal Infirmary. Mr Smith,
while he refrained from denouncing the project outright, certainly
seemed to be doing his best to pour cold water on it. He said he
wished it to be understood that the directors of the infirmary were by
no means indifferent to the claims of sick children – only the other
day they had acquired 12 new cribs for their young patients. In his
view, one objection to a children's hospital was that it was necessary
to admit mothers along with very young children – and this had
proved such a difficulty in the children's hospital in Edinburgh that
it had been found necessary to bar children under two, the very age
group in which mortality was greatest. After observing that Glasgow's
high infant mortality rate was partly accounted for by its high birth-
rate, Mr Smith concluded his speech, perhaps a trifle unconvincingly,
by assuring his listeners that he was not saying these things to
discourage the present movement.

The Rev. Dr Norman Macleod, the celebrated brother of Dr
George Macleod, rose to refute him. There were cries of 'Hear, hear'
when Macleod said that he placed greater confidence in Dr John
Cowan's opinions on matters of this kind than in Mr Smith's, and
that the experience of many other cities proved Dr Cowan correct.
Similar cries of approval greeted Cowan himself when he claimed
that it was not within the infirmary's power to admit children to the
extent necessary. The meeting, undeterred by Mr Smith and his
prophecies of doom, went on to approve the resolution to establish a

children's hospital; and before the gathering dispersed several handsome subscriptions had been promised.

But the opposition had scarcely started. Medical opinion was still mixed on the subject of children's hospitals. When the Medico-Chirurgical Society of Glasgow held a debate on the proposed hospital, opinion was almost unanimous that there was no need for specialised institutions of this kind.

Medical theory, however, was perhaps not the only motive behind the opposition of the Royal Infirmary. Its managers had reason to fear that a children's hospital would channel off charity hitherto received by their own institution. Nor did they waste any time in stating their case. In March, 1861, *The Glasgow Herald* published the report of a special committee set up within the infirmary to investigate its provision for children. This stated that 171 children had been treated in the infirmary in the previous year and claimed that 'in no case is any patient refused admission on account of age.' The report promised that increased accommodation for children could be provided in the infirmary 'if it were felt to be a want in the community;' and it added, somewhat crushingly, that children at an infirmary could be dispersed among the wards 'to obviate the acknowledged evils arising from the collection of great numbers of children together.'

The promoters of the children's hospital counter-attacked swiftly. Their reply to the Royal, signed by eight doctors associated with the movement, soon appeared in the *Herald*. The first signatory, through the accident of alphabet, was Dr A. D. Anderson of the Royal Infirmary – who had actually sat on the committee responsible for drawing up the infirmary's own report. A dissenting member of that committee, he had afterwards written a letter to the editor of the *Herald* accusing the Royal's directors of riding roughshod over the views of others and of trying to gain a monopoly in the treatment of diseases of all kinds. John Gibson Fleming, another outstanding physician at the Royal, was also a signatory of the report replying to the Royal, as was Dr Robert Scott Orr, secretary of the proposed hospital.

Their report pulled no punches. As well as accusing the infirmary directors of having 'gone beyond the limits of their office' in this matter, it castigated them for failing 'to announce any decisive arrangements for the treatment of children at all. . . while they endeavour to damp the zeal of those who are desirous of supplying the unquestioned and crying want.' It poured scorn on 'the recent introduction of a few cribs into wards already overcrowded' and it disapproved of 'the exposure of such sensitive patients to the atmosphere of so large a hospital as the Infirmary, and to the moral as well as physical taint which they are subjected to in its wards.' The authors of the report expressed astonishment 'that the Infirmary directors, knowing how inadequate the hospital accommodation, present or in prospect, is for the wants of this growing city, especially in epidemic times; knowing as they do how the medical officers are constantly compelled to dismiss these lighter cases to make room for the graver; knowing how crowded the wards often are, should wish to increase the confusion and augment the existing evil by still further encumbering the apartments by inserting cribs for children in the small space which intervenes between the beds for adults.'

This was a powerful counterblast to the Royal; and the promoters were backed by some influential allies. *The North British Daily Mail* launched an investigation into children's hospitals in Paris, London, Manchester, and other cities, emerging with information which 'fully convinced us of the unfounded nature of the outcry which had been raised in opposition to the movement.' A few years later the *Mail* contemptuously recalled 'the foolish opposition offered by some of the directors of the Infirmary, who imagined that, by affording another channel for the receipt of the alms of the charitable, the funds of the Infirmary would suffer to a corresponding extent.'

But the arguments, however impressively marshalled, were all in vain. Mere words could not prevail against the influence of the infirmary. The battle Royal was over, for the time being at least. For a month or so the promoters soldiered on, canvassing subscriptions – the £1,000 mark was passed that spring (though the outbreak of the American Civil War, which was to have a calamitous effect on the city's trade, hardly promised well for the future). But a meeting called on May 1 was poorly attended and only perfunctorily recorded in the minute book. There were to be no more meetings for four years.

Chapter 3

CROSSES AND VEXATIONS

THERE were some new faces when the movement renewed itself in 1865, and before long there was a new leader. Andrew Macgeorge, who became secretary of the movement (and later of the hospital itself) emerged as its dominant personality and most militant advocate.

Macgeorge was a well-known personality in Victorian Glasgow. The son of a solicitor, he had enrolled at Glasgow University at the age of 11, and at 15 was apprenticed in his father's office. Noted in legal circles for the zeal with which he advanced the interests of his clients, Macgeorge was also formidable as an ecclesiastical lawyer – with a taste, as someone put it, for clerical imbroglios. 'He always enjoys,' it was noted, 'a tussle on the subject of the Kirk.' Passionately interested in religious matters generally, he regarded the Church of Scotland as the embodiment of ecclesiastical perfection and was a pillar and a power within it. No General Assembly was complete without Andrew Macgeorge. All other branches of Christendom were anathema, not least the Free Church of Scotland on which he launched an energetic assault in his volume of *Papers on the Principles and Real Position of the Free Church.* But his brother, as one Glasgow journalist observed, remained 'in the outer darkness of dissent', being Episcopal Dean of Argyll and the Isles.

A tall, spare man with handsome, clean-cut features, Macgeorge was in his mid-50s when the movement for a children's hospital revived itself in 1865. He had a silvery voice, a dignified manner, old-fashioned courtesy – and a capacity for wading through enormous amounts of work without apparent fatigue.

'A capital specimen of one of our few literary lawers,' declared one of his contemporaries. The law and the Church – and the children's hospital – by no means exhausted Macgeorge's energies. He was an authority on history (the author of *Old Glasgow*), on archaeology, and on heraldry, finding time to write *The History and Use of Flags* and to draw attention to heraldic shortcomings in the coinage of the realm.

Andrew Macgeorge as portrayed in the 'Bailie'.

'It would be vain to say he is a universal favourite,' commented *The Bailie*, a Glasgow journal, in an article on Macgeorge, 'but he can safely be left to defend himself.' He proved also a most formidable defender of the movement for a children's hospital, unleashing on those who stood in its way the polemical powers at other times directed against his ecclesiastical opponents.

★   ★   ★

When the hospital promoters regrouped themselves for action in April 1865, it was resolved to push ahead 'without further delay' and collect the sums subscribed during the earlier movement – and to look out for a building on lease. Within a year £2000 had been collected, and at the end of 1866, a Grand Bazaar was organised by 'ladies in Glasgow and the neighbourhood who took a warm interest

21

in the subject', some £3000 of the proceeds going to the proposed hospital. There was, however, a setback at the end of 1867, when it was decided that 'in consequence of the great commercial depression which at present prevails it would be hopeless to make the general appeal to the public for subscriptions which has been for some time proposed'.

But worse was to come. In 1861 the promoters had fallen out with the directors of the Royal Infirmary; this time they were to fall out with the Senate of Glasgow University.

In 1870 the university removed itself from the Old College in the High Street to Gilmorehill; and as a condition of the government grant towards the new buildings it had undertaken that a hospital to serve the west end of the city should be built nearby. For a while, in the late 60s and early 70s, after much to-ing and fro-ing behind the scenes, the promoters set their sights westwards, in the confident hope that the children's hospital would be built on the same site as the new infirmary. Later they were criticised for having been too ambitious; and it is certainly true that the hospital would have opened its doors far sooner if there had been no deviating from the original plans for a more modest and central site. On the other hand, there were excellent reasons for wishing to establish the hospital near the university. The initiative, moreover, appears to have come from Gilmorehill itself; according to the records of the movement 'various parties interested in the university' prevailed upon the promoters to delay their search for a city site. And the plans, ambitious or not, came very close to success. At one time it seemed practically certain that the children's hospital would be built near the Dumbarton Road entrance to the university – where, very likely, it would have remained to this day.

The Senate had approved the idea in principle and, after a three-year delay resulting from complications in the siting of the Western Infirmary (originally destined for south of the River Kelvin), made a definite offer in 1872 to place part of the infirmary ground at the disposal of the promoters. The condition of the offer – that the children's hospital should provide clinical instruction for students – was only too willingly accepted, for it was this very consideration that had made a site near the university seem attractive. A site was offered, inspected, and accepted; terms were agreed to and set forth in a missive; only the signatures had still to be added.

Then things began to go wrong. For months no word was heard from the university's law agent although Macgeorge wrote to him 'again and again'. Eventually the agent wrote to say that it was 'out of my power' to reply to the letters. Then in April 1873, Macgeorge received an equally cryptic communication from the law agent – who enclosed, without comment, an excerpt from a Western Infirmary minute which stated:— 'In respect of the Senate's decision the Committee of the Western Infirmary cannot proceed further with the negotiations.' The promoters 'after some difficulty' – which can well be imagined – obtained a copy of the minute of the relevant Senate meeting, at which it had been resolved that it was *ultra vires* to convey the ground to anyone distinct from the university or the infirmary. The manoeuvres on Gilmorehill were fairly complex, but what appears to have happened is that many members of the Senate had earlier been under the impression that the children's hospital was to be an adjunct of the infirmary – and backtracked when they realised that it was to be an independent institution.

The reaction of the promoters may be imagined. Later, in a report to their subscribers, they were to speak of 'the extraordinary conduct of the Senate' and of its 'refusal to implement an arrangement to which the faith of the university stands pledged.'

Macgeorge, furious, launched into another angry round of letter-writing. This time the target was W. T. Gairdner, Professor of Medicine and former M.O.H. of the city, who had led the negotiations on the Senate side. Macgeorge wrote to him demanding an explanation and expressing the views of the hospital's executive committee at the Senate's decision – 'to say they were surprised would not in any way express the feeling with which they received it.' Gairdner was thus somewhat unfairly being made a scapegoat for the Senate – he himself had backed the project from first to last – and in his reply he declined to be held responsible for their doings. To a further hostile letter from Macgeorge he replied coldly and in formal terms, stating: 'I have washed my hands of the business.'

Nevertheless the Senate, whether on Gairdner's initiative or not, made one more move: they offered to provide a site for the children's hospital if it were placed 'formally in connection with the Western Infirmary for the purposes of clinical instruction'. But once more Macgeorge had to apply 'again and again' for written details of the proposal. When these finally arrived, two years later – the delay

23

resulted from boundary adjustments to the infirmary grounds – they were found 'inadmissable both as regards the site and the conditions'. The site, as a result of the boundary adjustments, was considered too small, and the conditions were presumably thought to leave the hospital too little independence. Negotiations stretching over a decade had gone for nothing.

The delay had not gone unnoticed in the press. 'We have heard nothing for a long time of the proposed hospital for sick children,' commented *The North British Daily Mail* in 1870. The *Mail* claimed that Glasgow's infant mortality rate could be cut in half by better sanitary conditions – 'but,' it added, 'even in the best regulated of our crowded cities there must always remain room for an hospital devoted solely to children's disease.' One reason for this, the paper pointed out, was the importance of studying such diseases, for 'a disease in a lecture looks altogether different from a disease in a patient'. The nursing of children in a general hospital was also the subject of controversy in the correspondence columns of both the *Mail* and the *Herald*, with one letter-writer alleging that nurses in a general hospital were 'as unfit to nurse a sick child as a bear is to nurse a canary bird'.

★　　　★　　　★

Having broken off diplomatic relations with the Senate, the promoters now began to cast about for a suitable building on a central site. The search was led by James T. Whitelaw, a Glasgow merchant who had been associated with the movement since 1870 and who later, as the first chairman of the directors, was to be an indefatigable worker for the hospital until his death in 1886.

Whitelaw and his committee were 'most particular in their choice of a site'. In the course of 'inquiry in every likely quarter' a promising-looking dwelling house, the property of a Mr David Anderson, was found high on the north slope of Garnethill at the corner of Scott Street and Buccleuch Street. The site 'afforded from its elevated position, every facility for a perfect system of drainage, is airy, in immediate proximity of a large working class population, yet so near to the west-end as to be easily accessible to the ladies who may naturally be expected to take an interest in such an institution and to exert themselves on its behalf.' After a thorough going-over by Macgeorge and Whitelaw the house was pronounced suitable and in 1880 was purchased for £2000.

The hospital at 45 Scott Street. The sculptured façade still survives in 1972.

The crosses and vexations which had for so long been endured by the promoters were not yet at an end. A large number of neighbouring proprietors opposed the venture – unsuccessfully, but at the cost of further delays.

Clearly, Mr Anderson's house would need considerable alterations and additions to tailor it to its new purpose. James Sellars, architect of the recently opened St Andrew's Hall, was appointed for the task and soon set off with James Whitelaw to tour children's hospitals in England 'in order that the most modern construction and appliances might be seen.'

The principal considerations kept in mind were 'perfect drainage, freedom from damp, good ventilation, and an equable temperature.'

In the interests of economy the work was all done by contract 'with responsible tradesmen'. The cost of the hospital, including site, furnishing, and equipment, was £12,510 10d – not all of which had been paid by the time it opened. The construction of the extension was not free from the frustrations that had beset the whole enterprise thus far – delay was caused when a large well was discovered during the digging of the foundations.

As the hospital finally – unbelievably, it must have seemed to the founders after their long years of frustrated effort – neared completion, the time came to draw up a constitution. This entrusted the government to a board of directors elected by the subscribers to the hospital, though during its first year it was run by a committee of management. The objects of the hospital were also set forth:— to provide treatment for children of the poor suffering from non-infectious diseases or accidents and to set up a dispensary for advice and medicine; to 'promote the advancement of medical science with reference to the diseases of children' and provide instruction for students; and, finally, 'to diffuse among all classes of the community, and chiefly among the poor, a better acquaintance with the management of children during illness, to educate and train women in the special duties of children's nurses, and to instruct lady pupils in the care of sick children.'

A 'large and influential gathering' attended the formal opening in the Corporation Galleries on December 20, 1882. Principal Caird of Glasgow University addressed the assembly in his rich, resonant voice. Archbishop Charles Eyre, a Yorkshire man who had become Roman Catholic Archbishop of Glasgow at a time when it was considered undiplomatic to appoint either a Scot or an Irishman, was also present. So was Dr Marshall Lang, successor to Norman Macleod at the Barony Church, active supporter of the sanitary reform movement, and later principal of Aberdeen University. Other clerical speakers included the Rev. Albert Goodrich, who wondered why there should be children's hospitals 'even in Constantinople and such places of false philosophy,' but none until now in Glasgow; and the Rev. Dr Henry Drummond, who made reference to 'the many, many little graves and fondly kept sprinklings of soft hair.' It was the Rev. Marcus Dods of Renfield Free Church who, on this highly inter-denominational occasion, moved the resolution 'that the Glasgow Hospital for Sick Children now to be opened is an institution deserving the sympathy and liberal support of the city and the west of Scotland.'

After the ceremony the company walked up to the little hospital – still empty of patients – and 'inspected it minutely, the completeness of the arrangements exciting universal approval.'

Chapter 4

GARNETHILL

THE first patient, a five-year-old boy suffering from mild curvature of the spine – which was successfully treated – entered the Glasgow Hospital for Sick Children on January 8, 1883. From then on 'the wards gradually filled up as the hospital became known'.

The patients, aged from two to 12, and clad in day and night dresses made by the ladies of Hyndland Church, occupied three wards (two medical and one surgical) in the new extension. Much thought had been given to their surroundings. The wards, one on each floor, fronted Buccleuch Street and because of the dreary urban outlook the windows had been painted – 'at considerable expense and with artistic effects,' wrote one physician – to reproduce Randolph Caldecott's illustrations of nursery rhymes: *The Babes in the Wood, Sing a Song of Sixpence*, and, on the top floor, *The House that Jack Built*. In the interest of hygiene the lower part of the ward walls was lined with 'tiles of an agreeable cream colour, with a narrow red border'. Attached to each ward was its own scullery and bathroom. The cots, 58 in all, had elastic wire mattresses.

In addition to the three main wards there was an isolation ward, separate from the hospital proper, and much used in those days of rampant infectious diseases. The nurse detailed to attend infectious cases occupied a little room attached to the ward and did not return to the hospital 'until all danger is past'.

A broad staircase, with richly coloured stained glass windows, marked the junction of the new extension with the original building, which was used principally for administration. On the ground floor of Mr Anderson's old house was the reception room, where patients

The hospital on Garnethill. The two lower storeys on the left of the entrance are part of David Anderson's old house.

were examined by the house surgeon, and next to it the reception bathroom where they were cleaned and clothed in ward uniform. 'The preliminary bath,' noted Andrew Macgeorge, 'is usually a formidable thing, and the exclamation, "Oh, I'll be drooned," is not uncommon with children whose acquaintance with water has been very slight.'

Adjoining the older building, on the opposite side from the wards, were the mortuary and the post-mortem room. The mortuary, which was the gift of James Whitelaw, had been designed on the principle that such places should be 'not repulsive and dismal, but decorous'. The floor was of marble mosaic and round the walls ran a dark grey wreath-patterned frieze with the words, 'Not dead but sleepeth.' The

29

room had an amber light with a white star cut on it, and palms and a crown of thorns were sculptured on the outside of the door. Relatives could if they wished have the child's funeral from the mortuary, and a service there instead of at home.

A 'plentiful supply of water, free of charge' had been kindly laid on by Glasgow Corporation water commissioners. In addition to the latest methods of heating, lighting, and ventilation there was some noteworthy gadgetry. The hospital boasted an impressive Victorian intercom system – speaking tubes enabled the matron, from her sitting room and bedroom, to communicate with the wards, kitchen, laundry, and (no doubt sometimes to the irritation of the occupants) the nurses' and servants' quarters. (Later the chairman of the directors ordered a telephone, 'which he thought would prove useful.') There was also 'an ingenious contrivance' specially invented for the hospital which ensured that the coal hoist, after delivering its load, locked itself up before children could clamber into it. Plans for a lift for patients had been abandoned on the advice of 'various medical gentlemen', no doubt in the interests of safety.

The speaking tubes have long since vanished, but the building still stands, and above the entrance a sculptured relief of mother and child remains as a reminder of its former purpose. Though the portal may seem fairly elaborate to modern eyes, the converted building was seen at the time as 'plain, inexpensive, and in keeping with its surroundings'. Today, more than half a century after the last patient vanished from Garnethill, the layout of the wards can still draw admiration from senior members of the Yorkhill staff. James Sellars had done a good job.

★　　　★　　　★

The nurses, housed at first in an extra storey built on to the original house, were responsible for more than just nursing. 'The Sisters, as well as the nurses, probationers, and pupils, are all ladies,' proudly announced the hospital authorities. 'Experience has shown that educated gentlewomen are more conscientious in the fulfilment of their duty, not only in attending to the wants of their little charges, but in instilling good manners, gentleness, and better moral principles than their home teaching has afforded.'

It is perhaps not surprising that the directors made such a

production of all this. Florence Nightingale and her lamp had now replaced Sarah Gamp and her bottle of gin as the symbol of British nursing – the idea that this could be a serious profession had spread rapidly from the Crimea to civilian life. But Florence Nightingale's influence did not immediately reach Scotland, and though her pupil, Mrs Rebecca Strong, had been installed as matron of the Royal Infirmary since 1879, it was not so long since nursing had been regarded as 'the last refuge of female adversity'.

The nursing staff was responsible for maintaining a high moral and religious – though inter-denominational – tone in the hospital. Evening prayers were said by a Sister and repeated by the children, and grace was sung before meals. 'It is very touching', the authorities found, 'to see the attenuated hands reverently clasped, and to hear the voices of the convalescents around the table, and the sick in their surrounding cots, join in this simple invocation.' On Sundays nurses read Bible stories to the children, and 'such appropriate books as are sent to the Hospital'. There were also – 'as in all well-regulated hospitals' – morning and evening prayers for the nurses. The gong that summoned them to prayers at 7 a.m. was also the signal that the children were free to talk – 'a privilege', as Andrew Macgeorge noted, 'which they are not slow to indulge.'

The 'pure moral atmosphere' of the hospital would, the managers were confident, later 'do something to cheer many a wretched home'. The tale was often told of the little boy who on his return from hospital started to teach his brothers and sisters to sing grace; unfortunately he had forgotten the words, and his mother had to call at the hospital for a copy of them.

Besides nursing the children and maintaining the moral tone of the hospital, the nurses were also responsible for such domestic chores as polishing the ward floors. This they continued to do until the task was taken over in 1904 by 'two charwomen who were thoroughly respectable and well-known in the Hospital'.

The matron – or Lady Superintendent as she was at first genteelly called – also had wide-ranging responsibilities. In making this appointment the promoters had followed four guidelines:

'1. That it is desirable that an educated lady be appointed.
'2. That she be experienced both as a Lady Superintendent and as an Housekeeper.

'3. That if she had had experience of work in a children's Hospital a preference be given.

'4. That her age be from 30 to 40 years, not exceeding the latter.'

There were 34 applicants. On a visit to England Dr J. B. Russell, medical officer of health for Glasgow and for many years a director of the hospital, interviewed several of them. On his return a short leet of three was drawn up – a Miss Robinson of London would have been a fourth but Dr Russell 'mentioned that he had seen that lady and recommended her not to think further of the appointment as the climate of Glasgow was not suitable for her health'. He had also gone to Leicester Infirmary to see Mrs Louisa Harbin, formerly of Great Ormond Street Hospital, 'and was very well pleased with the cleanly and orderly state of her wards. . . . Mrs Harbin's personal appearance and manners were agreeable.'

Mrs Harbin was offered the job at £84 a year plus board, lodging, and laundry expenses. She accepted, promising in somewhat canny terms 'to abide by any rules which shall be made in the future and possible for me to carry out'.

Louisa Harbin was to remain at the hospital – once receiving leave of absence to visit her son in Florida – until her early retiral in 1903. Responsible for the housekeeping as well as for the wards, she was also expected to act as unofficial security officer – as is illustrated by an odd episode early in the hospital's history. The cook was one day apprehended by the police as she left the hospital, bearing with her some of its property. She and her husband, an unemployed labourer who 'got his dinner frequently at the hospital', had often been seen leaving the premises with suspicious-looking parcels and had also, it emerged, brought special containers for carrying away milk. The cook was given 14 days and Mrs Harbin, evidently held responsible for the incident, was given a stricter security code to enforce. Years later she turned the tables by presenting the board with her own memorandum on 'Things which have lapsed in the Royal Hospital for Sick Children'. The things lapsed included, for example, the advance notice given to surgeons of patients being prepared for operation.

★　　　★　　　★

Visiting days were on Wednesdays and Sundays, an hour on each occasion. Before setting foot in the wards visitors were obliged to remove their boots – a rule which was revoked only in 1909 after 'a strong protest against this practice as being unnecessary and not a little offensive to parents'. No such practice, it was noted, existed at the Royal and the Western; and at the Victoria Infirmary visitors were issued with sandals.

Sometimes there were more serious problems in the relations between hospital and parents. There was, for example, early in the hospital's history, the couple who insisted on removing a critically ill child from hospital. When a nurse later sought out the home she found 'a little room without an article of furniture, and on the floor, covered by dirty shavings, lay the poor dying Teddy'.

One mother went to the opposite extreme. 'You seem to be fond of my wee bit wean,' she is reported to have said to the Sister who was holding the child. 'If ye like tae keep it a'thegither I'll gie't tae ye, and ne'er speer after't ony mair. I hae nine o' them.'

Chapter 5

THE FIRST DOCTORS

GLASGOW now had a children's hospital; it still had no children's doctors. The term 'paediatrics' did not come into common use until the present century; and although the importance of the diseases of childhood had long been recognised – the first treatise in English was Thomas Phaire's *The Boke of Chyldren* in 1545 – the subject emerged as a specialisation only at the end of the nineteenth century.

Britain was a late developer in this respect, lagging behind Austria, Germany, and the United States – at the opening of the twentieth century there were only three paediatricians in the country. This was largely because of the organisation of hospital work. The medical and surgical staffs of children's hospitals were composed of men from the major general teaching hospitals who gave only a small part of their time to the care of children; at Garnethill, as elsewhere, the honorary physicians and surgeons would each visit the hospital only two or three times a week, their major hospital work being in the infirmaries. Also, being unpaid for their hospital work, they had to rely on private practice among adults for their livelihood – and inevitably tended to focus their interest on those diseases of older children with which they were already familiar in the adult. 'The realisation', in the words of one present-day paediatrician, 'that infants and young children differ greatly from adults in their metabolic processes came slowly and only when some men began to devote their whole time to paediatric practice, often at great financial sacrifice.' That time was still well in the future when Garnethill opened.

There were some glittering names among the visiting staff when the little hospital opened. The honorary surgeons were William Macewen and Hector Cameron; the honorary physicians James Finlayson and William Leishman. An extra-honorary physician and an extra-honorary surgeon stood in for them when necessary.

Macewen and Cameron were to remain the hospital's surgeons till the early 90s, working away in the little gas-lit operating theatre on the top floor, with its glass cupola roof, its tiled walls, and its side window which was 'useful for passing a current of fresh air over the operating table'.

Macewen and Cameron had contrasting personalities and different approaches to surgery; procedure in the operating theatre would vary according to which one was in charge. Cameron, who had been Lister's house surgeon when carbolic acid was introduced at the Royal Infirmary and remained his life-long friend and disciple, would carry out his operations in strict accordance with the antiseptic principles of surgery. Macewen, though he too had been Lister's house surgeon and had practised Listerian principles, had by now moved on to an even more recent method, aseptic surgery. There would be much preliminary washing of hands under running water and boiling of gauze for swabs and dressings when Macewen was in charge; and he would also grace the little Garnethill hospital with a white coat – still a novelty at that time. (Lister had worn an old rubber apron smeared with carbolic.)

Macewen's period at Garnethill largely coincided with the years when he was revolutionising the whole practice of surgery, including brain surgery, through his work at the Royal Infirmary. 'A dynamo of industry regulated by genius' is how his biographer, Dr A. K. Bowman, has described him. In his mid-30s when he first appeared at Garnethill, Macewen was a man of towering stature, bearded, and with piercing steely blue eyes. Brusque, inclined to use the royal 'we', inspiring enthusiasm in most house surgeons and terror in some students, he was an interesting contrast to his surgical colleague at Garnethill, Hector Cameron.

Sympathetic in manner, though he could also be firm, Cameron was a highly popular man with magnetic personal qualities and a great fund of anecdote. *The Bailie*, by no means a sycophantic journal, once described him as a beau ideal doctor. 'Dr. Cameron,' it commented, 'while one of the most expert and daring, is also the least shoppy of surgeons.'

35

Cameron, a few years older than Macewen, had been born in Demerara, where his father was a well-known sugar planter (his own son, Hector Charles Cameron, was to be an eminent twentieth-century paediatrician). Sent home from British Guiana to be educated in Scotland, he was for a while a fellow student of Andrew Lang in the Arts Faculty of St Andrews University. His medical studies took him to Glasgow University – where, later, he was to become Professor of Clinical Surgery. During his years at Garnethill he also worked at the Western, and was at one time surgeon to

Hector Cameron

almost every public institution in Glasgow. He remained associated with the children's hospital as an extremely vocal honorary vice-president long after he had ceased to serve it as visiting surgeon.

Both Macewen and Cameron received knighthoods, but this was for their work at the infirmaries rather than at Garnethill. They were not paediatric surgeons, and the range of operations on young children was still limited. In the early years at Garnethill tracheo-stomy – the creation of an artificial airway to relieve children choking from diphtheria – was the commonest emergency operation, and it was merely a palliative procedure, bringing about few recoveries.

36

Osteotomy, the bone-straightening operation pioneered by Macewen, was certainly performed at Garnethill. In the first year of the hospital's history 12 osteotomies were performed, which meant removing a compound wedge of bone to correct bow-legs and knock-knees caused by rickets. Nevertheless it was at the Royal Infirmary, some years before the children's hospital opened, that Macewen had perfected the technique of this revolutionary procedure; and it seems highly unlikely that he was responsible for much pioneering surgery at Garnethill. Dr A. K. Bowman, asked for his views on the subject, commented: 'From the absence of positive information in his published work, and even in his personal and private records, I have felt bound to believe that, during the nine years when he was a visiting surgeon to the Sick Children's Hospital, little operative work of particular significance was carried out by him at Garnethill. Facilities in respect of both surgical accommodation and equipment were primitive, and the only reasonably good arrangements at his disposal were those which, through his own exertions and in the midst of the most unprepossessing surroundings, he created for himself at the Royal Infirmary. It would have been contrary to his whole nature had he embarked on much elective [or non-emergency] surgery in the children's hospital, and I fancy that his practice there would be centred upon such emergencies as occurred – fractures, for example, together with empyemas, threatened blockage of the respiratory tract, and so on.' Nevertheless, Dr Bowman added, the children's hospital had a most important role to play as a provider of material; children would be referred to Macewen there, and later admitted to the Royal to be operated on for brain abscesses and other disease.

★   ★   ★

The name of James Finlayson was not the most famous one on the early visiting staff, but in the context of the hospital's history it is the most significant. Just as, a little later, James Nicoll was to be a forerunner of the paediatric surgeons, so Finlayson foreshadowed the paediatricians of the twentieth century – and perhaps does not always receive due credit for his pioneering in this field. Though there could be no real paediatricians until there was an opportunity to pursue the subject full-time, general physicians could nevertheless develop a special interest in sick children; and James Finlayson did so.

A former pupil of Glasgow High School, Finlayson had spent several years in business before turning to medicine (he was to become a leading authority on medical insurance). Alone among the early visiting staff he came to Garnethill with specialised experience of children's diseases; his first post had been as house surgeon at the Clinical Hospital and Dispensary for Children in Manchester. Returning to Glasgow he worked at the Royal and later at the

James Finlayson

Western, and when the children's hospital opened he was a natural choice for the post of visiting physician. During his years at Garnethill he became recognised as one of the chief Scottish authorities on children's diseases. Had it been possible in those days for a physician to do his principal work at the children's hospital instead of at the general ones, there is little doubt that James Finlayson would have chosen to do so; and the study of child health would have benefited accordingly. Even as it was, Finlayson's published works – which were voluminous – included a treatise on teething difficulties and several important papers on children's temperatures in health and sickness. He was indeed a pioneer in clinical thermometry, and his

first paper, 'The Normal Temperature of the Child,' pointed out the diagnostic value of an evening rise in temperature.

Heavily built, hen-toed, slow of speech and movement, Finlayson was calm and deliberate in all he did. His painstaking attention to detail is revealed in his unpublished memoranda on various aspects of the children's hospital. Some considered him 'one of the most valuable assets that the medical school possessed'; others found him ponderous. 'The action of his brain appeared at times to be sluggish,' wrote J. Walker Downie, who was not only Finlayson's colleague at the Western but also the honorary aurist at the children's hospital. The man's solemn demeanour, suggested Downie, together with his Biblical lore, 'was probably the ground on which a one-time rumour rested that the university Senate proposed to confer upon him the honorary degree of D.D.' Finlayson was in fact an active Congregationalist, though less interested in theology than in working through the church to improve the conditions of poor children. He was one of the promoters of the children's convalescent home opened in Eaglesham in 1890 by Trinity Congregational Church in association with the children's hospital.

A life-long bachelor, he was a scholarly man, browsing through medical literature in French and German and interesting himself deeply in medical history. For a quarter of a century he was the honorary librarian of the Faculty of Physicians and Surgeons of Glasgow, and his account of the founder, Maister Peter Lowe, is well known in medical circles. It was Finlayson who represented the faculty at Queen Victoria's funeral, and later, attempting to describe the scene to the assembled Fellows, he 'became so affected that tears ran down his cheeks, and his voice failed him'.

On social occasions Finlayson could discard his solemnity and sparkle with good humour. Clad in his grey tweed suit and bowler hat he would 'border on the frolicsome' when he joined fellow-members of the Western Medical Club for a country excursion. Gentle, kind to patients, he was characteristically painstaking as a teacher and had 'a strong belief that the proper place for a student to learn his work was at the bedside'. He was cautious in his use of drugs, and strong on dietetics. 'I have visions of him', wrote one of his former students, Dr Freeland Fergus, 'with a pot at the ward fire giving us practical demonstrations as to the making of beef tea and other foods suitable for patients.' Fergus, who was oculist for a time

39

at the children's hospital, also recalled Finlayson's alarming habit of asking an unwary student to write a prescription; sometimes the prescription would be made up and the prescriber invited to take, literally, a dose of his own medicine. When, inevitably, the student found it to be 'a horribly nauseating compilation', he was lectured on 'the impropriety of ordering mixtures which invalids could not possibly be expected to take'.

★   ★   ★

Finlayson's fellow physician at Garnethill, Samson Gemmell (who almost immediately replaced Professor Leishman on the visiting staff) was not a specialist in children's diseases in the same sense as Finlayson; but he served the children's hospital for many years and after his death his name became linked with paediatrics through the Samson Gemmell Chair of Medical Paediatrics, established at Glasgow University in 1924 in his memory.

Gemmell, who became Professor of Clinical Medicine at Glasgow University in 1908, was an Ayrshire man with a superb sense of humour and wide-ranging interests which included history, poetry, and archaeology. One of his most distinguished former students, the late Lord Boyd Orr, described him as 'the man with the widest outlook on medical and world affairs generally that I have ever met'. He recalled in his autobiography how Gemmell, lecturing to his students on infectious diseases at a time when these were on the decline, would launch into an off-the-cuff but profound exposition on Buckle's *History of Civilisation*. 'I learned more philosophy from him', commented Boyd Orr, 'than in my official philosophy class.'

Other famous figures who flitted in and out of the little hospital included Joseph Coats, the first Professor of Pathology at Glasgow University, who was honorary pathologist for the first decade of its history. Robert Muir, his successor in the Chair, also became pathologist at Garnethill. As well as an honorary pathologist there were, when the hospital opened, an oculist, an aurist, and a dentist, who attended 'when their services are required, as the Directors may arrange'. There was no anaesthetist till 1901; until then anaesthetics were administered by the house surgeon. Chloroform was almost always used, with ether only in exceptional cases.

The house surgeon was the only resident medical officer when the hospital opened, but he was joined some years later by a house physician, and the resident staff remained at this strength till the turn of the century. Some of the young housemen in those pioneering days on Garnethill were later to become long-serving and distinguished members of the visiting staff. R. H. Parry, house surgeon in 1886 and 1887, was still serving the hospital as consultant surgeon half a century later; and Barclay Ness, who in 1889 became the hospital's first house physician, is still vivid in the minds of many who worked at the hospital after the First World War.

Chapter 6

UNFUSSY PHILANTHROPY

THE little operating theatre on the top floor was the scene of 68 operations in the first year of the hospital's history. Four years later the annual total was more than 200, and whereas in the first few years medical cases had outnumbered surgical ones the pattern was reversed as a somewhat greater variety of operations became possible. 'Lives are saved by skilful interference and patient nursing in cases which formerly were refused or discharged as incurable,' reported the directors. 'By the same means limbs are preserved which would have been summarily removed.' One result of the increase in surgical patients was the reduction of the mortality rate in the wards to 6·6 per cent, since fewer surgical cases were fatal.

This was excellent in itself; but the low proportion of medical patients was worrying. Medical – as opposed to surgical – diseases were the principal cause of the city's high infant mortality rate, and this had been one of the main justifications for opening a children's hospital. The trouble was that parents, especially before the opening of an out-patients' department, were usually readier to bring children needing surgical, rather than medical, treatment to the hospital. The number of surgical patients and their longer average residence also brought accommodation problems, and in 1886 it was decided that some of the overflow should occupy vacant cots in one of the medical wards.

This infuriated James Finlayson. Having been at some pains to arrange for medical students to visit his ward he was more than somewhat put out by the fact that, when they did arrive, the ward was full of surgical patients. Such cases, he maintained, did not differ significantly from those treated in a general hospital, whereas the practice of the medical wards was essentially different. (Finlayson was a stout participant in that traditional tug of war between physicians and surgeons. Twenty years later, canvassed for his views on the proposed new hospital building, he roundly stated: 'The real requirements of a *special* children's hospital are for medical, not surgical cases. The general bulk of surgical cases are tubercular joints and bones, and the provision for these should undoubtedly be in the country.')

By the mid '80s the shortage of space was becoming really serious. In its first year the hospital had treated 260 patients; in 1886 there were 458. Lists of patients who had been under treatment for more than two months were regularly submitted to the directors and 'the attention of the staff was directed to the dismission of these patients as soon as they seemed to have obtained all the benefit which hospital treatment could confer'.

Lack of space affected everyone. While James Finlayson was protesting that his ward was overcrowded, and doing elaborate calculations in cubic centimetres to prove it, Mrs Harbin was complaining about the cramped quarters for nurses. 'I don't think you are fully aware *how* cramped we are for bedroom space,' she wrote to a member of the board. 'We have only the exact number of *beds* and two rooms have three beds.'

When the house next door in Buccleuch Street came up for sale there could be no dithering over the decision to buy it. It was purchased for £1500 and plans were made to convert it into a ward and 'commodious dormitories' for staff. Money was short and it looked as if the plans would have to be shelved till better times. But Thomas Carlile, who had become chairman of the board in 1886 after James Whitelaw's death, stepped forward and offered to foot the bill himself – and to pay £200 annually for three years for the maintenance of the new ward. Altogether he contributed £1700.

The ward – L-shaped, 'nicely heated and lighted,' and with 12 cots – was named after Carlile. It was thanks to his generosity, *The Bailie* commented, that 'poor little sufferers from our back lanes and alleys have a haven and refuge, a place of healing, where they are more carefully nursed and tended than they possibly could be if even these hours of illness were spent in the most luxurious nurseries of the West-End'. This seems to have been fairly typical of Carlile, a man

43

of retiring disposition and charitable impulse. 'There is nothing about him of the fussy philanthropist,' said *The Bailie*. 'There is probably no man so usefully engaged in charitable work in Glasgow whose name is less paraded before the public.' He was a Paisley man, a partner in a Townhead chemical works, and a patron not only of

Thomas Carlile

hospitals and sick children but of art and artists. It was Carlile who had been the recipient of Finlayson's lamentations about the overflow of surgical cases into his ward, and this appeared to weigh heavily with him. The new ward, devoted to surgical cases, would put an end to this infiltration without, as he put it, 'placing any check on the surgical work which is now carried on with so much success.'

       ★   ★   ★

If Garnethill suffered from that chronic problem of hospitals, shortage of space, at least it did not suffer from shortage of nurses. Applicants for training as nursing pupils were so numerous that many had to be turned down. Students, too, were beginning to come about the wards, even if they hardly arrived in droves. The first seven students enrolled in 1885, paying a guinea each for the privilege; and thus a start was made to realising one of the fundamental objects of the hospital.

Two years later there came encouraging 'evidence of the fact that the Hospital has established its position as an important field for medical research'. The local branch of the British Medical Association forsook their customary haunts, the Royal and the Western, and held their annual meeting at Garnethill. The B.M.A. gave the hospital exactly a week's warning of their intention, but whatever feelings of incipient panic may have accompanied the preparations the event seemed to go off well enough. 'The arrangements for the accommodation and entertainment of our members were admirable,' wrote a B.M.A. representative in his bread-and-butter letter. It had been a fine piece of publicity for the hospital.

Chapter 7

VICTORIAN FUND-RAISING

THE hospital remained a voluntary one until the coming of the National Health Service; but it was never more voluntary, or voluntary in a greater variety of ways, than in those early years on Garnethill. Not only the finances of the hospital but also much of its social and welfare work depended on volunteers.

One reason for the choice of the Garnethill site had been its accessibility to the prosperous women of the west-end. These 'benevolent ladies with time at their command', as James Finlayson described them, did more than busy themselves with money-raising bazaars and musical soirees. From the first the ladies' committee, drawn from the hospital's subscribers and their relatives, played a vital part in the life of the hospital, and their work took them into the wards of Gartnethill and the wynds and closes of the city slums. When a child was discharged from hospital one of the ladies' committee visited the parents, 'pointing out to them the necessity or desirableness of such a mode of treatment as their knowledge of the child, or the advice of the physicians or surgeons, may suggest.' The ladies' committee appointed an almoner when the hospital opened, but nothing is recorded of her work and she appears to have disappeared fairly rapidly from the scene; the burden of welfare work fell at first on their own shoulders. 'It is peculiarly a women's mission,' commented the directors, 'and is performed with a zeal which is beyond all praise.'

The committee also visited the wards in rotation, arranged for children to be sent to convalescent homes, distributed clothes to convalescents, and supervised 'all arrangements as to singing and reading in the wards'. They played an important part in fund-raising, with an annual door-to-door canvass (a system which also brought in money from other parts of the country).

These collections were not of course the only source of revenue. Money came from a variety of sources and was raised in an astonishing variety of ways. Regular subscriptions came from individuals and organisations, from factories and warehouses and businesses. Contributions flowed from churches, Bible classes, and Sunday schools; from a festival held by the Coachmen of Glasgow; from the collecting box in the refreshment room of Oban railway station. A Liverpool soap manufacturer sent £2 representing 'modified damages paid to him by a Glasgow firm of drysalters, against whom he had taken proceedings'. A Miss Fergus sent 16s collected by her St Bernard dog. The Anderston Weavers' Society had a whip-round for the hospital on board the Glen Sannox during their annual outing; the Theatre Royal sports at Hampden Park yielded £7; and in 1886 the sum of 3s 8d was 'collected at a Christmas dinner in Uddingston, after hearing a boy playing the violin'.

The Scottish Football Association were faithful supporters, regularly sending part of the proceeds of the Glasgow Charity Cup. Theatrical and musical events, professional and amateur, were another rich source of finance. The Orpheus Club gave £50 from performances of *The Pirates of Penzance*; the Philomel Club gave a concert specially for the benefit of the hospital; and at the Royal Princess Theatre £2 8s was 'collected in boxes during the visit of the Joe company'.

The lists of contributions offer glimpses into the social life of Victorian Glasgow. Money was raised at soirees and conversazioni, at lectures and sermons, at wild flower exhibitions, at a fancy dress ice carnival at the Skating Palace, and at a 'Sacred Concert' at the Scottish Zoo. Mr Vallance's Elocution Pupils' Entertainment yielded £1; a collection was taken at Professor Max Muller's 'gratuitous lecture on Toleration' in the Queen's Rooms, and another at Shandon Hydro after a service conducted by Canon de Molagus. The Western and Northern Grocers' Soiree Committee contributed, and so did Elgin Place Literary and Home Reading Circle, the Sedate Club, the Athenaeum Gymnastic Club, the Elmbank Stravaigers, Govan Rob Roy Four-in-Hand Club, Dennistoun Amateur Minstrels, and the Committee of Glasgow Coachmen, Grooms, and Friends.

47

Some gifts were anonymous – such as the contributions from 'Napoleon B.' and 'A Systematic Giver', or the 'offering from a working Woman, per Hermione'. Some hinted at stories untold – the money paid to avoid a slander action, and a 10s 6d contribution from 'the Committee of the 15th Annual Soiree of the Cork Cutters of Glasgow, being amount paid by a lady artiste to avoid legal proceedings for breach of engagement'.

Gifts came from parents of former patients – 'Thankoffering for Daisy', or, more clinically, 'Thankoffering from Parents on whose child Tracheotomy was successfully performed.' Children, too, contributed. A handsome gift of £14 came from 'Master Harry Thomson's Children's Bazaar, at 4 Berlin Terrace, Pollokshields'; and, more poignantly, a contribution of 2s represented 'Little James Leechman's savings (a patient)'. There was also a contribution from something called the Children's Bazaar and Café Chantant in Banff.

One patient, a blind girl who died of tuberculosis, even left a legacy to the hospital. 'It had been Nellie's great desire to leave something to the Hospital where she felt she had been treated with so much kindness, or to use her own expression "where a' the folk were awfu' guid to her", but her relatives were unable to carry out her wish. She was sure if her soldier brother returned from India that he would give her money for the purpose, and was always asking the Sister to look in the newspapers and see if his regiment was ordered home. The idea of leaving something took such a strong hold on her that Mr Macnaughton, the clergyman who visited her, mentioned it to her companions in the Asylum for the Blind, and at the Townhead Public School, and they collected £2 1s 7d and gave it to her on her thirteenth birthday that she might gratify her wish.'

There were also gifts in kind. Flowers came weekly from a mission in Bearsden, oranges annually from the Tharsis Copper and Sulphur Company. Lord Balfour of Burleigh sent pheasants, the Marquis of Breadalbane grapes, and the Marchioness of Breadalbane champagne. The Band of Hope in Cambuslang gave Christmas trees laden with toys. Sigismund Seligmann sent 24 pints of claret. A school sent an Easter gift of 400 eggs; someone subsidised a 'Pic-nic Nurses and Children to Mugdock Castle'; nurses were sent tickets for the Fine Arts Institute and Hengler's Circus. Gifts rolling in to Garnethill included a canary, an American organ, 'one globe and goldfish', a Chinese gong, a Union Jack, an Armenian cradle, pictures of the

Queen, a window garden, a cuckoo clock, dolls' houses, a see-saw, and a positive stampede of rocking horses.

If the impression remains that the children's hospital was a clamorous treasure trove of Chinese gongs and cuckoo clocks, with rocking horses outnumbering children, it should be added that many gifts were of a strictly utilitarian nature – calico and cod liver oil, semolina and cornflour, mowing machines and plaster of Paris. Fruit and vegetables were generously given – though a gentle request for 'not only rare and delicate fruit and vegetables, but also the commonest kinds' hints at who knows what exotic offerings of aubergines and capsicums. Clothes arrived in quantity – six dozen flannel jackets from Mrs Bottomley's sewing party, 14 pairs of shoes from the wife of the Lord Provost. Large parcels of knitted under-wear arrived each year from *The People's Friend*, the products of their annual knitting and sewing competition. *The People's Friend* were faithful supporters of the hospital; in 1887 they organised a 'Juvenile Wild Flower Exhibition' in Glasgow, and as a result of the money raised one of the hospital cots was named 'The People's Friend Cot'.

The naming of cots was a regular practice. Donors of £100 were entitled to name a cot, donors of £1000 could endow a cot and have it permanently inscribed, and those who gave £2000 could name a ward. Garnethill's cots included the Amateur Dramatic Club cot, the Philomel cot, the Magpie Minstrels cot, *The Weekly Herald* Guild of Kindness cot. The Sister Elizabeth cot was named in memory of one of the hospital's nurses; the Carrick Buchanan cot was named by the Lanarkshire and Renfrewshire Hunt, and the West of Scotland cot by the British Order of Ancient Free Gardeners. This system of naming cots continued until the end of the voluntary hospitals system. After the First World War many cots were to be named after soldiers killed in battle.

Annual subscribers to the hospital were allowed to recommend one patient for every guinea subscribed. It was ruled that in 'cases of competition in the recommendation of patients' preference be given to the most urgent case – and emergency cases could of course be admitted without the usual recommendation.

This system of subscribers' lines, which was commonly practised at the time, was described by one of the founders of the hospital, Sir George Macleod, as 'one of the banes of our present hospital system, and the direct cause of many deaths'. In practice, the hospital accepted cases sent in by any medical practitioner, the house surgeon later obtaining the necessary lines from one of the directors. Conversely, some cases sent in by subscribers were turned down as unsuitable for a hospital of this kind. But the very existence of subscribers' lines must often have been a deterrent.

★   ★   ★

'The Directors again earnestly plead for an increase in the number and amount of annual subscriptions' – every annual report contained a variation on this theme. The annual cost of maintaining the hospital was about £2500, and though at the end of the first year the initial debts had been paid off there remained only £300 in the bank – and this at a time when an out-patients' department was urgently needed. It was to raise money for this dispensary, and to establish a small permanent endowment for the hospital, that a great 'Fancy Fair' was held in the St Andrew's Hall in December 1884.

The Fancy Fair was quite something. 'Nothing like it has ever before been attempted north of the Tweed,' declared *The Bailie*, claiming that the entire west of Scotland was agog. The St Andrew's Hall had been elaborately got up as a fourteenth-century English market place with 'quaint old shops, red brick walls, tiled roofs, high-pitched gables, and latticed casements'. At one end of the hall stood the Town House, and at the other 'Ye Tabard Inn' occupied a prominent place on the orchestra gallery. Two rustic pavilions stood in the centre of the scene, and perched on one of them was a model of a well-fed chanticleer. 'An old dovecote and the village cross fill up little odd corners,' noted one observer a little helplessly.

The scenery was not the only striking feature. 'The general effect of the Fair was,' as the *Herald*'s reporter put it, 'heightened by the majority of stallholders, many of whom were attired in costumes peculiar to the natives of Continental countries.'

Clad in the costume of a Portuguese peasant, the Duchess of Montrose presided over an enormous stall 'composed entirely of rustic work' and with a garden in front and a maypole on either side. An assortment of countesses, and numerous 'great county ladies', took an active part in the proceedings; and the Lord Provost's wife presided, suitably enough, over the town house.

The contents of the stalls, like the costumes of the stallholders, ranged somewhat beyond the normal scope of fourteenth-century English market places. There were Japanese wall panels, Benares brasses, pottery from Constantinople, fans from Spain, Venetian metal work, Bombay pottery, Japanese armour, a picture painted by the Crown Prince of Germany – and clothes ropes and coal riddles. There was also a game stall where 'Sir George Leith Buchanan and various other gentlemen do the honours'. Fringe events included spirited amateur performances of *Alice, or the Woodman's Daughter* and a 'Demonstration, with Experiments of Light and Sound, by Professor McKendrick'.

It was, pronounced *The Bailie*, a grand fashionable festival, and those who supported it would 'do something towards brightening little eyes and easing throbbing temples and lightening heavy hearts'. Many did support it; and many must have left the St Andrew's Hall clutching coal riddles and Benares brasses, for the proceeds of the fair amounted to more than £15,000. Out of this sum £4000 was allocated to the site, building, and furnishing of a dispensary. An engraved tablet referring to the Fancy Fair can still be seen on the outside wall of the building which resulted.

Chapter 8

THE DISPENSARY

'I think the out-patients' department on the whole the best organised and most efficient I have ever seen in connection with any children's hospital anywhere,' wrote Henry C. Burdett, of *Burdett's Hospital Annual*, after a visit to Glasgow in 1892.

From the first it had been recognised that the hospital would be incomplete until it had an out-patients' department – there were those who would have given this priority even over the opening of wards. Obviously, the hospital itself could treat only a strictly limited number of children – about 500 a year by the mid-'80s. A dispensary on the other hand could treat thousands; and an added advantage in a children's dispensary was that small patients who were seriously ill could be carried there in their mothers' arms. A dispensary, it was thought, would direct to the hospital many children who would never otherwise have found themselves there; and in particular it was expected to act as a feeder to the medical wards. 'Medical diseases are the chief causes of infant mortality among Glasgow children,' commented the directors, 'and the poor require to be taught to avail themselves more readily of the help of the Hospital in such cases.'

The dispensary, unlike the hospital, was to be built from scratch. And there was to be a first-class row before ever it got beyond the drawing board.

A large site was needed, since in dispensaries it was obviously an advantage to have the maximum accommodation on the ground floor. The location was also important. Inquiries had shown that 'the north-western part of the city, including the large district of

Cowcaddens and Garscube Road and east and west of them up to the canal, stand most in need of an institution of this kind'. After much searching a 'very eligible site' was found within five minutes' walk of the hospital, at the east end of West Graham Street. After some haggling it was purchased for the steepish price of £2000.

The Dispensary in West Graham Street. The building is now part of the Western Region Hospital Board's department of clinical physics and bio-engineering.

Instead of appointing an architect in the usual way it was decided to hold a competition. Three leading city firms were asked to submit plans – Campbell Douglas and Sellars; John Baird and James Thomson; and John Burnet and Son. The designs submitted by James Sellars, architect of the hospital – and the successful candidate in a similar competition for the design of the Victoria Infirmary – won the day. They were, however, a trifle expensive, and since the ladies who had organised the Fancy Fair were adamant that their contribution to the dispensary should be limited to £4000, Sellars was asked to make modifications.

53

There was another worry. The honorary president of the hospital, Archibald Orr Ewing, M.P., disapproved of the designs. John Burnet, he thought, would have been a better bet than James Sellars.

Orr Ewing, who had been one of the leading promoters of the hospital, was laird of Ballikinrain, a farmer in the foothills of Ben Lomond, a Turkey red dyer in the Vale of Leven, a merchant in Glasgow, and M.P. for Dumbarton for many years. 'One of the typical Scotch members of the lower House,' someone once observed. He did not mince his words. James Sellars's plans were, he thought,

Archibald Orr Ewing as he appeared in 'The Bailie'.

expensive and unsuitable; the site ought to be reduced to street level; the rooms had 'too many angles and corners'. He voiced his objections to the architect, but considered the subsequent modifications 'of little consequence' – and proceeded to draw up his own, entirely different, ground plans for the dispensary.

These the directors rejected, stating that they were unwilling to start the whole business again from scratch. Orr Ewing was in London when he received this news, and from the House of Commons library he despatched a blistering letter resigning his presidency 'as I desire to have no part in directing his extravagant monstrosity'.

For good measure he withdrew his offer to contribute £100 towards the dispensary if nine others could be found to do the

54

same – 'and of whom,' he concluded scathingly, 'you have got none.'
A copy of his letter, no doubt to the annoyance of the directors,
appeared in the press.

The honorary president's actions, together with his description of
himself as 'the chief counsellor' of the hospital, and his insistence on
his right to summon board meetings, caused something of a consti-
tutional crisis. The directors wrote to Orr Ewing politely pointing
out that it was not in the text of the constitution (a copy of which
they enclosed) that honorary office-bearers, such as himself, should
be 'troubled with executive duties'. Orr Ewing declined to withdraw
his resignation and soon the directors decided to stop asking him.
The Duke of Montrose was elected president in his place.

If the dispensary failed to please Orr Ewing, it at any rate pleased
The British Architect. 'An excellent work in the twofold aspect of
artistic design and practical planning,' that journal declared. 'The
grouping and proportion of the exterior design are, to our mind,
singularly pleasing.'

In the entrance hall, where a fountain commemorated James
Whitelaw, the late chairman of the board, children were divided
into medical and surgical cases and passed accordingly through
separate doors into the reception hall. This was a spacious, airy room
with rows of benches on either side for each class of patient, and it
appears to have made a deep impression on some parents. 'The
mother', wrote Andrew Macgeorge, 'at the first visit often looks
round as if awestruck by "so grand a place", and on their return, as
one of the Sisters tells us, the more tidy and cleanly appearance of
both mother and child seems to show that the mother has been
"trying to make them more fit to be in it".'

After being called into the consulting rooms on either side of the
reception hall parents and patients emerged into a common hall in
front of the dispensary room, where they received their medicine
before leaving. The ground floor also contained an isolation ward
and the upper flat included a room for specialists and accommodation
for the dispensary Sisters.

★   ★   ★

'The sluggishness, inertia, and ignorance of the poor fall in a terrible
way on the children,' said Professor W. T. Gairdner at the official

The scene in the entrance hall of the Dispensary.

Awaiting their turn at the Dispensary.

opening of the dispensary in October 1888. 'The facts that we come across daily show the deplorable apathy that exists regarding the perishing offspring of the poor. Almost every medical man knows of cases in which parents, out of a family of 10, 12, or 14 children have lost one or two, and yet have actually come to think that it is in the ordinary course of God's providence, or at all events that it was an almost inevitable misfortune.' The very existence of a dispensary would, Gairdner said, help to correct this attitude among parents – 'even if they do not avail themselves of it they know it is there.'

Many did avail themselves of it. In 1889 there were 4000 cases – more medical than surgical – with a total of 16,000 attendances. Month by month the work increased, making an extension necessary within five years of the opening. By 1890 more than half the cases at the hospital were coming from the dispensary, and by the end of the century 7000 cases a year were being treated there. The nature of the cases treated showed that the dispensary was striking at the roots of child mortality in Glasgow. Almost half of the medical patients were treated for diseases of the lungs and nutritive organs – which were, the hospital authorites pointed out, 'unquestionably the main scourges of child life in Glasgow.' Bronchitis, pneumonia, diarrhoea, atrophy, debility, dyspepsia, and gastric and intestinal catarrh were the commonest ailments treated.

Subscribers' lines, to the great gratification of Sir George Macleod, were not needed at the dispensary – 'It is enough that the child is sick and poor.' To make sure that he was in fact poor as well as sick, cases were submitted to the scrutiny of the Glasgow Charity Organisation Society. This somewhat controversial organisation, which was sometimes accused of operating a system of espionage, had been set up in 1874 'to organise charitable relief and repress mendicity'. Soon, however, the officers of the society had satisfied themselves that the majority of patients were so obviously poor that investigation was unnecessary and thereafter only 'selected cases of an apparently doubtful nature' were referred to them. Many of the dispensary's patients came from homes where the wage-earner was temporarily unemployed or incapacitated from working. 'Many such cases would scorn to "come on the parish",' wrote Andrew Macgeorge. 'In such cases when a mother can, without loss of independence or self-respect, come to a dispensary like this at the very commencement of a child's illness, and get advice and medicine free, the good done is incalculable.'

In cold weather soup as well as medicine was dispensed; and at Christmas time more festive fare was provided. On Boxing Day, 1889, 100 patients were entertained to tea by the ladies' committee. The dispensary hall was 'tastefully decorated' for the occasion. Sadly, it was noted that there was 'an absence of the boisterous hilarity which characterises a meeting, say, of healthy Sunday school children, and the appetite of the assemblage was distinctly below par'. The magic lantern proved more popular than games since the party-goers were 'of a contemplative rather than of a romping disposition'. After these entertainments they were sent home 'happy in the possession of an orange and some toys' and sometimes with a petticoat or pair of stockings from one of the large consignments sent by *The People's Friend*. In later years Howard and Wyndham sent free pantomime tickets for the dispensary treat, and once at the turn of the century children were entertained in the dispensary to a performance by two acrobats from the Grand Theatre.

★   ★   ★

Unlike many other hospital dispensaries at that time, the one at West Graham Street had the services of full-time trained nurses. The two dispensary Sisters – the staff was later increased – played a vital and indeed almost heroic role in its history. After a morning in attendance at West Graham Street the Sisters sallied forth to spend the afternoon visiting the homes of out-patients – one taking the medical cases and the other the surgical. 'It is impossible', stated the directors, 'to estimate the benefit conferred on these poor children by their skilful hands, and also on the parents by their kindly hints and directions in the management of those numerous sick beds scattered about the closes of the poorest districts of the city.' The Sisters assisted with surgical dressings, gave medical advice and hints on 'the maintenance of domestic cleanliness and wholesomeness', and to the poorest homes they took milk, eggs, and beef tea.

The name of one of the dispensary nurses became a household word. Sister Laura, who worked at West Graham Street for many years, developed the original formula of the baby food still marketed under her name – a venture which somewhat distressed the directors at the time. It has been said, incidentally, that one of the hospital's physicians had a hand in the invention. Sister Laura must also have been a familiar figure as she went her way about the closes of Cowcaddens visiting the sick, for she is commemorated in a rhyming ball game:

> 'Sister Laura walks like this,
> 'Pit a pat pat, pit a pat pat.'

Sister Laura – Miss Laura M. Smith – worked at the hospital itself for five years before going to West Graham Street, and was Sister in charge of the dispensary for 30 years before she retired because of poor health in 1922. When Mrs Harbin retired in 1903 Sister Laura was one of 29 applicants for the post of hospital matron, and though unsuccessful reached the short leet of five. Soon afterwards 'as a mark of appreciation for Sister Laura's long and excellent service' her salary was raised from £40 per annum to £60 – nearly double the normal salary for a Sister. When she retired the chairman of the board referred to 'the unique character of Sister Laura's work at the dispensary and the way that she has spent herself unsparingly in carrying on that work, and for the welfare of the immense number of out-patients who had passed through her hands'.

★   ★   ★

In the entire history of the dispensary, from 1889 to 1953, one name stands out – James Nicoll, who was visiting surgeon there for 20 years.

It was an age of brilliant Scottish surgeons, and James Nicoll was one of the most brilliant of them all – some have rated him second only to Macewen. Though his career was incomplete – he died in his mid-50s, never having fully recovered from a bout of dysentery in France during the First World War – it included pioneer work in many fields, notably brain and abdominal surgery. He was surgeon to the Western Infirmary, Professor of Surgery at Anderson College, and had a large private practice; but the children's hospital was no mere sideline. Nicoll was a man ahead of his time, and it was at West Graham Street that many of his most radical ideas were put into practice. He can properly be judged a forerunner of the paediatric surgeons.

The son of a Free Church minister, Nicoll was born in the burgh of Hillhead and educated at Glasgow Academy and Glasgow University; and his visits to foreign medical schools took him as far as Moscow. He was just touching 30 when he became visiting surgeon to the children's dispensary, and working at West Graham Street between 1894 and 1914 he operated on an immense number and variety of cases (more than 7000 over one 10-year period), many of them of a type not previously considered suitable for out-patient treatment. At the dispensary he boldly demonstrated that, given perfect technique, hernia and spina bifida cases could well be cured by out-patient treatment. Cleft palate operations on suckling infants

James Nicoll

could also, he proved, be successfully performed at a dispensary – and between 1899 and 1901 he performed no fewer than 406 operations for hare lip and cleft palate. He also pioneered a two-stage plastic operation for pyloric stenosis – obstruction of the stomach outlet – which significantly reduced the mortality rate.

Nearly half the patients treated by Nicoll at this period were under three years old, and many of these were under one. Though he conceded that among older children there were cases unsuitable for dispensary treatment, he maintained that 'in children under two years of age there are few operations indeed which cannot be as advantageously carried out in the out-patient department as in the wards, and, while the number increases with each year, the increase is not great until the age of five is reached'. Many cases being treated in the wards were, Nicoll argued, a waste of the hospital's resources since 'the results obtained in the out-patient department at a tithe of the cost are equally as good'. Moreover, infants in the wards were 'noisy and not infrequently malodorous' and the notion that they rested quietly in their cots after an operation was 'a pretty idea, rarely obtainable'. After a dispensary operation, on the other hand, 'such young children, with their wounds closed by collodion or rubber plastic, are easily carried home in their mothers' arms, and rest there more quietly, on the whole, than anywhere else.' Nicoll's experience at the children's dispensary gradually brought him round to the view that adults, too, were often kept too long in bed after an operation, and in his wards at the Western Infirmary he worked towards the reduction of the recumbent period to less than a week.

Nicoll attached immense importance to the part played by the mother in the recovery of an infant. Weaning a baby after an operation could be dangerous, he stated, and even bottle-fed babies might be harmed by separation from their mothers. Nicoll was a man who believed in getting things done even if it meant dipping into his own pocket; and on his own initiative – and to the indignation of the directors when they discovered – he went ahead and rented a house near the dispensary where out-patients and their mothers could be accommodated after an operation and attended by dispensary nurses and doctors. When the new hospital was being planned at Yorkhill he strongly advocated that provision should be made for nursing mothers – no children's hospital, he maintained, could be complete without this. A ward at Yorkhill was in fact equipped for this purpose, with glass screens between the beds to keep parent and child separate from other patients while allowing them to see what was going on; but because of shortage of space after the First World War it was not used for its original purpose, though on rare occasions a mother was accommodated at the hospital.

'No doctor', said a colleague of Nicoll's, 'impressed himself more on the imagination of the public of Glasgow.' He was a man of great charm and grace, liked by colleagues, nurses, and patients – 'children were devoted to him, as he to them,' it was remarked. When he was Professor of Surgery at Anderson College students contested for the front seats; and at the dispensary it became necessary to construct a new lecture room for his clinic. Once he officially represented the interests of students – as assessor to President Poincaré when he became Rector of Glasgow University. When Poincaré returned to France after the rectorial installation he described Scottish students as the most brutal in Europe – but he awarded Nicoll the cross of the Legion of Honour.

Nicoll, who was a bachelor, never allowed himself the luxury of a long holiday. But though work appeared to be the most important thing in his life he had many outside interests. On country walks he 'proved himself well informed in the life of birds and keenly alive to all varieties of natural beauty'. Art was another interest, and one room of his house was specially decorated for the display of etchings by Whistler and D. Y. Cameron (a life-long friend), while a group of Hornel paintings hung on the walls of another.

★   ★   ★

Many distinguished names were associated with the dispensary. John Lindsay Steven, an outstanding pathologist at the Royal Infirmary and earnest advocate of temperance, was one of the first members of the visiting staff. Another member was Charles Workman, also of the Royal Infirmary, who combined a vast store of assorted knowledge with an inability to summon up the right fact at the right moment – 'Workman', said a colleague, 'was a fine fellow but he had lost the index to his mind.' J. Hogarth Pringle and John M. Cowan were among other notable names on the dispensary staff. The latter once contributed to a serious staffing problem in West Graham Street: his service in the Boer War coincided with the absence of Dr Alfred Webster, who was caught up in a different kind of battle on the home front – fighting the bubonic plague, which broke out in a small way in Glasgow in 1901. A substitute was found for Webster 'till he is freed from his plague work'.

In addition to James Nicoll such well-known surgeons as Farquhar Macrae and Alfred Young worked at the dispensary. Young was a member of the surgical staff from 1898 to 1914, also becoming surgeon in charge of the hospital's country branch when it opened in 1903; and when the new hospital opened at Yorkhill he was visiting surgeon there from 1914 to 1920.

Dr Alice McLaren, the first woman medical practitioner to

become established in Glasgow, was also on the dispensary staff. The daughter of a Leith merchant, she was educated at Cheltenham Ladies' College and the London College of Medicine, where she became the first woman to receive an M.D. Returning to Leith to work in the general hospital, she became the first woman to be appointed an honorary physician in any British hospital; this she followed up by becoming the first woman to be appointed to the visiting staff of a Glasgow hospital – the Samaritan. Alice McLaren, who was in her 30s when she became an extra honorary physician at the children's dispensary, was also one of the founders of the Redlands Hospital for Women, where she became senior gynaecologist. Her pioneering spirit led her to become associated with a group of Glasgow women interested in social remedial work, and she took a keen interest in the women's suffrage movement.

Long-serving members of the dispensary included Barclay Ness and J. B. MacKenzie Anderson, who were later to become honorary physicians at the hospital proper. It was Ness who, in 1901, took over the battery massage cases and other electrical treatment at the dispensary. This was a fairly important job, since high hopes were then held in the curative powers of electricity through galvanic stimulation – 'the Frankenstein syndrome', as one modern doctor has called it. On one occasion Ness put in an unsuccessful request for an electric bath.

Barclay Ness also found himself at the head of various delegations from the dispensary staff to the hospital authorities. One such delegation agitated for more accommodation to be provided both at the dispensary and the hospital, since space was so short at Scott Street that many out-patients found to be in need of hospital treatment had to be sent elsewhere. The directors sympathised, but said two facts had to be reckoned with – 'the one that there were no funds available; the other that there was no space.'

Other doctors had a more fleeting connection with West Graham Street. In 1902, for example, a Surgeon Captain Murray of the Indian Civil Service was appointed assistant at the dispensary for two months while he was home on leave.

Working on the upper floor of the dispensary were the specialists – a dentist, an aurist, an oculist, and, after a Röntgen Ray apparatus had been presented to the hospital at the turn of the century, an honorary medical electrician.

The dentist appears at first to have had rather limited scope. In 1901 Mr Rees Price, who had been honorary dentist since the opening of the hospital, asked the directors for 'the necessary apparatus for the filling of teeth'. This, he reckoned, would cost about £3, plus a further £5 'if a Drilling Machine were provided'. Price explained that 'at present he had only the appliances for removing teeth, and that if the Directors granted his request he could save teeth which at present he could only draw'. The request was, mercifully, granted.

The era of James Nicoll and Sister Laura was the heyday of the dispensary, but it continued to do valuable work till its closure in 1953 (after 1914 out-patients were also received at the new hospital at Yorkhill). Today the building in West Graham Street – with the name 'Sick Children's Hospital Dispensary' still carved on the wall – houses part of the clinical physics and bio-engineering department of the Western Regional Hospital Board. But a long Cowcaddens tradition has died hard. A few years ago the physicist to the Board, Dr J. M. A. Lenihan, wrote that the building 'still sees a few mothers and weans wandering wide-eyed among the Geiger counters, seeking vaccination or balm for bruised limbs'.

Chapter 9

TOWN AND COUNTRY

THERE was a change of name in 1889, when the hospital was given permission to add 'Royal' to its title. And as well as a royal name there were royal visitors – Princess Louise (sixth child of Queen Victoria), in 1888, followed by her elder sister Princess Christian in 1892. On her informal visit to Garnethill Princess Louise 'chatted kindly to the sick children' – and received from one little girl a bookmark which she had embroidered with the words, 'No cross, no crown.'

In 1897 the Queen's Diamond Jubilee was celebrated in style at Scott Street. The wards were decorated, tea and cakes were laid on by the ladies' committee, and everyone from the matron to the youngest out-patient was presented with a commemorative medal.

As the century drew to a close students began appearing in greater numbers on Garnethill. They also attended the dispensary, where practice among children could be better learned than in the wards; but the regulations had to be made more stringent after the discovery that 'three ladies who had enrolled as students at the dispensary were without any preliminary medical training, their object being to go abroad as missionaries'. After that only registered medical students were allowed to enrol.

Students from Queen Margaret College made their appearance at the hospital in 1892 – though they were not quite the first women students at Garnethill; two or three women from the London Zenana Medical College had received instruction there as part of a residential course in Glasgow. But female emancipation received a few rebuffs in these years. In 1900, after inquiries from intending applicants, the directors 'decided in the meantime that the positions of House Surgeon and House Physician, and Assistant Surgeon at the Dispensary, should not be open to women'. The reaction of Dr Alice McLaren is, alas, unrecorded.

The question of electing women to the hospital board also cropped up when communications on this subject were received from a body known as the Glasgow and West of Scotland Association for the Return of Women to Local Boards. This association received a somewhat dusty answer, being informed by the directors that 'the hospital already has the benefit of work done by a large ladies' committee who take an active interest in the affairs of the hospital'. But soon the ladies' committee were taking up the matter themselves, and after an alteration to the hospital constitution in 1901 two members of the committee were always on the Board.

★   ★   ★

The opening of the Carlile ward in 1887 had by no means solved the accommodation problem. In 1894 a new wing was added to the hospital, and the Carlile ward transferred to it. The flat roof of the new building was used as a playground, with easy access from the new ward below and the older ward next to it; garden seats and awnings were placed on the roof, and shelter was afforded by a large glass house with dark blinds. The house that had formerly contained the Carlile ward was converted into a nurses' home and 'the building, being separate from the wards, rendered the apartments more healthy, and in every way more suitable'. Nurses were also accommodated at the dispensary after an extension had been made there in 1897.

An important new departure in 1903 was the opening of a country branch at Drumchapel. Surrounded by trees on high ground near Drumchapel Station, the branch was built with a £6000 gift from Mrs Margaret Montgomery Paterson, of Edinburgh, in memory of her parents. There were two large wards, each with 12 cots, and much importance was attached to 'giving the patients all the fresh air and sunshine possible'. Patients could be taken from the lower ward into a large sunroom, and from the upper ward on to the sunroom roof, which was surrounded by a parapet. But it was not entirely a life of leisure; soon it occurred to the ladies' committee

66

that 'a little regular work' would do the patients no harm, and arrangements were made for two teachers to visit the branch twice a week.

Every Friday afternoon children were ferried between Garnethill and Drumchapel either by landau or by a private bus with a pair of horses. At Drumchapel they were treated by doctors from the dispensary led by Alfred Young, the surgeon; and a certain Sister Chris, who had previously worked at Garnethill, was put in charge of the branch under the general supervision of the hospital matron. The nature of the ailments – notably tubercular disease, especially of the hip joint – meant that the children's stay at Drumchapel was often quite prolonged. But the country branch was not intended as a convalescent home. Patients remained there only as long as they needed active medical or surgical attention, and sometimes minor operations were performed.

As well as giving the children the benefit of country air the new branch somewhat relieved the pressure on the wards at Garnethill. James Finlayson, for one, saw this as a breakthrough in hospital administration. It might, he thought, 'give a clue for the solution of the problem of hospital extension in Glasgow on other plans than the massing of sick persons in high, many-flatted buildings in a crowded urban locality.'

The country branch still thrives, even if the actual countryside has disappeared. Since the closure of the West Graham Street dispensary 20 years ago it has been the oldest section of the hospital still in use.

★   ★   ★

As the hospital grew older its patients tended to be younger. At first infants under two were expressly excluded – though exceptions were made for accident and other emergency cases. In the first year there were only 10 patients under two, but the number steadily increased. Ten years later there were 83, and by the end of the century about a fifth of the patients had not yet had their second birthday. Official policy lagged some way behind actual practice, for in 1901 the directors, concerned about 'the excessive number of babies under two in the hospital', told the medical chiefs to keep the numbers as low as possible. The number of babies in any ward at one time was then officially limited to three – a restriction which T. Kennedy

Dalziel, then the hospital's senior surgeon, strongly opposed. 'It seems to me,' he said in a letter to the directors in 1904, 'that the *raison d'être* for the existence of the hospital is to treat such patients who are not and cannot be admitted to a general hospital. . . . I think it would be better to admit fewer between 6 and 12, and take in more under two years – that is, if the hospital is to fill a real want.'

The want was certainly very great. The sanitary reform movement in the last third of the nineteenth century had dramatically reduced the city's overall death rate, but there had been no corresponding

The country branch at Drumchapel.

decline in infant mortality. During the last two decades of the century the rate had actually increased.

This is not as surprising as it may at first seem. Even the improvement in adult health has to be seen against the background of massive deterioration during the earlier part of the century; it has even been suggested that despite the improvement, the general health of the city was no better at the beginning of the twentieth century than at the beginning of the nineteenth. The sanitary movement, though dramatic, could not in itself bring about Utopia, especially in the absence of good housing; and the children of the poor still spent their first desperately vulnerable years in appalling conditions.

No one has described these conditions more vividly and perceptively than one of the hospital's own directors – Dr James B. Russell, who as Glasgow's second medical officer of health had successfully guided the late-Victorian sanitary reform movement through its final phase. Internationally recognised in his day, Russell deserves to be – but seldom is – remembered as one of the greatest men in Glasgow's history. He was no desk-bound administrator or armchair sociologist; his work took him constantly into the poorest quarters of the city, and it was with the advantage of extensive first-hand experience that he wrote an account, in 1886, of life in Glasgow's single-ends – houses which, as he pointed out, produced an enormous proportion of child deaths.

'There they die,' he wrote, 'and their little bodies are laid on a table or on a dresser, so as to be somewhat out of the way of their brothers and sisters, who play and sleep and eat in their ghastly company. From beginning to rapid ending the lives of these children are short parts in a continuous tragedy. A large proportion enter life by the side door of illegitimacy. One in every five who are born there never see the end of their first year.'

Russell, who once remarked that it would be safer to fall asleep at the foot of a tree in Central Africa than at the foot of a lamppost in the Bridgegate, gave the following gruesome account of childbirth and child-death in such areas:

'You go into one house and you find that twins had been born a few hours ago, and a knot of neighbour women sit round the bed, and the mother and her friends are alike maudlin with whisky. You go into another home where at your last visit you saw a child very ill, and you see the mother huddled up on the top of her bed sleeping in a drunken sleep, and you know that the child is dead. They baptise with whisky and they bury with whisky.'

If whisky was one source of infantile mortality another and more important one was, ironically, milk. It was scarce, often adulterated, and inadequately stored. The children's hospital had its own share of milk problems; J. B. Russell seemed continually to be testing the supplies – finding, for example, the level of boracic acid to be 'perfectly intolerable'; and tenders were frequently changed as one supplier after another proved unsatisfactory.

Poor milk caused not only tuberculosis but infantile diarrhoea – so prevalent that it was known as the summer plague. Even when the quality of the milk posed no direct threat to health the growing practice of bottle-feeding caused many deaths, because of the

Outside the country branch early in its history.

difficulty of ensuring adequate nourishment. Sir Hector Cameron, former surgeon of the hospital and subsequently its vice-president, pointed out that the great bulk of medical ailments in infants was caused by faulty diet. It was, he remarked, unfortunate that the human animal in its infancy was the only one 'deprived in a very large measure of the divine food which was provided for it, the maternal milk'. Dietary difficulties were not confined to the poor; in the early years of the twentieth century a sharp rise in infant mortality in suburbs like Pollokshields and Kelvinside was attributed to the spread of bottle-feeding and deficiencies in the accompanying diet.

Obviously the children's hospital had a great potential part to play in grappling with these problems. The trend of the times was on Kennedy Dalziel's side when he urged the admission of more babies. It was now becoming medically possible to treat many cases hitherto regarded as hopeless. Children's hospitals all over Britain and America were making provision for small infants, and it was inevitable that Glasgow would do the same. In these circumstances the official restrictions on babies were lifted, and in the latter years at Garnethill, before 1914, about a third of the patients were under two. Provision for many more was meanwhile being included in the plans for the new hospital on Yorkhill.

The problem was not static. Infant deaths from respiratory and digestive diseases were falling off, and at the beginning of the twentieth century new welfare measures – notably the establishment in 1904 of a Glasgow infant milk depot with advisory services – were helping to lower the infant mortality rate as a whole. But mortality in the first three months of life remained a stubborn problem; deaths from immaturity were increasing, and this was related to the severe problem of still-births and miscarriages. Dr A. K. Chalmers, Russell's successor as medical officer of health for the city – and, like him, a director of the children's hospital – attributed these early deaths not to disease but simply to the physical unfitness of the newly born to maintain an independent existence. 'For the most part', he said, 'they are the deaths of those who in a literal sense may be born to die.' No paediatrician would accept this pessimistic explanation today.

Many more of these extremely young infants were finding their way into the wards of Garnethill. This meant extra nursing and extra expense; but it also meant that the children's hospital was 'more and more fulfilling its true mission – a work which could not well be carried on in a general hospital', as the annual report for 1912 stated. In that year the hospital treated 440 patients under two years of age, and well over half of these were under 12 months. More than 100 were under six months, and of these 20 suffered from various moribund conditions and 15 from a progressive wasting condition known as marasmus, whose cause was still unknown. Marasmic infants rarely recovered in these days, but progress was being made in other fields; and in 1915 Hector Cameron said at the hospital's annual meeting that he had no difficulty in singling out the medical and surgical treatment of young children as the department of medical practice that had most conspicuously advanced in the previous 10 years. Physical, chemical, and bacteriological investigation was making diagnosis easier and more certain – less dependent on intuition and experience and less vulnerable to the old difficulty of non-communication between doctor and very young patient.

The rôle played by the children's hospital was in some sense missionary as well as medical. One of the hospital physicians, Barclay Ness, pointed out in 1910 that by far the most common cause of illness in the hospital patient was the ignorance of the mother. It was only, he added, in so far as they succeeded in teaching her to care for, feed, and bring up her children properly that any real and lasting benefit could be conferred on the patients.

The older children continued, in those years before the First World War, to be afflicted by rickets, pneumonia, broncho-pneumonia, and tuberculosis – which could affect joints, bones, brain, peritoneum, glands, lungs or spine. These years saw con-siderable efforts, both social and medical, to improve the health not only of infants but of all children – one impetus to improved public health standards being the large number of Boer War volunteers turned down as unfit. The routine medical inspection of school children was introduced nationally at the beginning of the century; and at the first inspection in Glasgow, in 1904, it was revealed that more than half the children found to be unfit had not seen a doctor.

Deficient diet, of course, affected older children as well as babies. John Boyd Orr, who in 1902 taught in a school in the city slums, later described the conditions:

'The rooms were overcrowded, and the children ill-clad,' he wrote. 'Looking back now, I realise that many of them were suffering from malnutrition and some of them from actual hunger. Some came to school with no breakfast, and others with only tea and bread and butter. Going round between the seats one could see the lice crawling on their heads and on their clothing. We were supposed to teach them grammar, arithmetic, and all the other subjects in the edu-cational curriculum. I went home the first night feeling physically sick and very depressed. I had another look at the school the next day, and came to the conclusion that there was nothing I could do to relieve the misery of the poor children, so I sat down and sent in my resignation.'

The remedy for such problems was social rather than medical; but medically there were some encouraging straws in the wind. The importance of the study of children's diseases was beginning to be recognised by the medical profession, and in 1900 the Society for the Study of Children's Diseases had been formed in London. (An older society was the Children's Clinical Club, a select band of about a dozen consultants whose earliest members included James Finlayson of Glasgow as well as the famous John Thomson of Edinburgh.) Glasgow, it is true, still had no full-time paediatricians, and the little hospital on Garnethill was hardly equipped for research. But as plans went ahead for a new building on Yorkhill the day was coming nearer when Glasgow would play a pioneer role in the treatment of children's diseases.

Chapter 10

NEW CHIEFS

SAMSON GEMMELL was the only one of the old guard of visiting chiefs still at Garnethill when the hospital entered the twentieth century. James Finlayson had recently resigned his post, though he was still sometimes called in as consultant; and by 1894 Macewen and Cameron had been succeeded by T. Kennedy Dalziel and Robert H. Parry, who were to remain the hospital's surgeons for the rest of its Garnethill days.

Kennedy Dalziel was one of the outstanding surgeons of his time, and at the children's hospital he played a dominant role, taking a very active part in the plans for the new hospital at Yorkhill. He was a Dumfriesshire man, and a graduate of Edinburgh University, and during most of his Garnethill years he was a surgeon at the Western Infirmary, where his skill in diagnosis and dexterity in operations were so well known that surgeons frequently travelled from a distance to see him operate. Though he was not a close reader of medical literature Dalziel continually surprised his colleagues with the extent and variety of his knowledge of current surgical opinion; this he was able to do through an uncanny habit of acquiring information by, as he himself put it, picking other people's brains. He was knighted in 1917, after serving as consultant surgeon to the War Office in the First World War.

A big, genial, hospitable man, Kennedy Dalziel was a farmer as well as a surgeon – few other medical men have had an obituary tribute to them written by the agricultural correspondent of *The Glasgow Herald*. A farmer's son, he had never lost his hankering for the soil and eventually acquired the estate of Nether Kinneddar, near Dunfermline, cultivating one of its five farms himself. The mansion house on the estate had once belonged to Lord Kinnaird, Court of Session judge and close friend of Sir Walter Scott, who had made many visits there; and the writing desk in the drawing room, where Scott had written several of the Waverley novels, was the object of frequent pilgrimages by Scott clubs.

Dalziel's own farm was said to be a model of its kind; and certainly he was in his element farming it. Friends noted that when he was out on the land all traces of the professional man left him. 'Out with his gun, or in the fields with a companion or two examining the shorthorns, or leaning over a ring side, watching the allocation of prize cards, he looked a stalwart gentleman farmer,' observed one of them.

Even in his professional rôle he cannot have appeared as a highly sophisticated man to his colleagues at the Western and Gartnethill. Lacking the urbanity of, say, Hector Cameron, he was plain and unassuming, strong in character and presence, and with, so it was said, 'much of the massive simplicity that goes with real greatness.' Someone who had been at the mercy of his surgeon's knife afterwards remarked that 'he inspires you with such tremendous confidence even when he says very little'. Sometimes, however, he had much to say, and said it in forthright fashion – urging the admission of more babies to the wards, for example, or declaring in public that he felt 'almost inclined to quarrel' with the directors for not planning more beds at the new hospital at Yorkhill.

One of Dalziel's oddest assignments in his days as senior surgeon at Garnethill concerned adults', not children's, disease. In 1905 there occurred at the country branch, in among the more expected outbreaks of scarlet fever and mumps, an apparent epidemic of appendicitis among the nursing staff – no fewer than five were operated on in less than a year. It fell to Kennedy Dalziel to investigate 'this somewhat remarkable circumstance' – which he put down to 'pure coincidence'.

Robert H. Parry, Dalziel's fellow surgeon at Scott Street, was a lively Welshman of bustling energy and arresting personality, rapid and versatile in his thinking. Though he lived in Scotland for the greater part of his long life, he never lost his Welsh accent or, as someone put it, 'the nervous energy of his race.'

The son of an excise officer, Parry had come to Glasgow to study

75

at the Royal Infirmary medical school, where he was strongly influenced by William Macewen. He obtained the Scottish Triple Qualification in 1885 and went into general practice in Hull. But his potential had not gone unnoticed in Glasgow, and when the new Victoria Infirmary opened in 1890, Parry – though he was only 32 and did not have a university degree – was appointed one of its surgical chiefs. (The other was A. E. Maylard, also still in his 30s, who worked for a time at the children's dispensary.) In his three decades as a chief at the infirmary Parry became widely known as 'a surgeon of delicacy in manipulation and precision in technique controlled by exact anatomy and sound pathology'. He was no specialist – shying away only from brain surgery and becoming expert in the neurological surgery of the limbs and in all that pertained to orthopaedic treatment. His consideration for patients was shown in his technique for excising glands from the neck through an incision behind the ear. The point of this operation was that Parry 'wanted not only to remove the disease but in so doing to leave no mark which might give rise to morbid feeling'.

As well as being one of the most sought-after surgeons of his day Parry was among the most popular teachers in Glasgow. His tutorial classes in surgery and his Saturday morning clinics were described as 'scenes of lucid exposition and of masterly display'. To these occasions he brought not only a scientific spirit but an artistic temperament which gave him a special facility in the demonstration of cases – 'anomalous gaits and postures and deformities he could imitate to perfection.'

Parry's association with the children's hospital lasted for more than half a century. He was resident medical officer at Garnethill in 1886, visiting surgeon from 1894 to 1914, and honorary consultant to Yorkhill until his death during the Second World War.

★   ★   ★

Samson Gemmell, with his off-the-cuff expositions on the history of civilisation, had an erudite colleague in George Middleton, who became visiting physician at the hospital at the turn of the century. Middleton had a first-class honours degree in Classics from Aberdeen University, and late in his life one of his colleagues 'found him reading with enjoyment Gibbon's *Decline and Fall of the Roman*

Empire, chuckling over the Latin notes at the foot of the pages in the edition he was perusing'.

Middleton had been a visiting assistant at Garnethill for many years before he joined Gemmell as full physician on James Finlayson's departure in 1898. His main work was at the Royal Infirmary – where he won a reputation as 'an all-round physician and an unerring diagnostician' – but he was also very much at home at Garnethill. 'It was perhaps here among the little ones,' wrote one of his colleagues, 'that Dr Middleton's kindness and sympathy were seen at their best, for he was characteristically Scottish in nature and dreaded showing his feelings.'

Bearded, bespectacled, and with bushy eyebrows, Middleton was in his mid-40s when he became a physician at the children's hospital. 'Old George was the hairiest man I ever saw, except for his bald head,' wrote O. H. Mavor, otherwise James Bridie. 'Hair luxuriated from every other square inch of his face and overhung his steel spectacles. He wore a little black alpaca jacket and carried an old wooden stethoscope. He talked in a high-pitched, testy old man's voice and kept strictly to the point.' Middleton was one of Garnethill's life-long bachelors, along with James Finlayson and James Nicoll. From nurses, housemen, and students he won great devotion, and his teaching was so gifted that some colleagues and former students persuaded him to start a class for their special benefit.

Gemmell and Middleton were succeeded in due course by two of the hospital's former housemen, Barclay Ness and J. B. MacKenzie Anderson, who were the last honorary visiting physicians before the hospital moved to Yorkhill in 1914.

Barclay Ness, who still came about the hospital as honorary consultant after the First World War, is affectionately remembered by those who knew him then as a little, plump, good-humoured man – 'less argumentative than some of the others,' one doctor recalls. He had worked at the dispensary before joining the hospital's visiting staff, and though his most important work was done at the Western Infirmary he was one of the first physicians in Glasgow to become interested in paediatrics.

A headmaster's son, he was educated at Glasgow Academy and Glasgow University, taking an arts degree before his medical one. As well as working at the Western Infirmary for more than half a century, he was associated with many other hospitals both through his teaching and his work in medical administration; he was also a professor at Anderson College of Medicine, and a president of the Royal Faculty of Physicians and Surgeons of Glasgow. Ness – who, incidentally, always scorned the use of an overcoat – had been one of the hospital's first housemen, and continued to serve it as honorary consultant long after he had left the visiting staff. Before his death in 1954, when he was in his 90s, he was probably the last contemporary link with the hospital in its earliest years.

The tall, handsome figure of J. B. MacKenzie Anderson presented a contrast to Ness's plump presence. Like Ness, he was educated at Glasgow Academy and Glasgow University, and like so many of his contemporaries had afterwards studied on the Continent. Later he became visiting physician at the Royal, and lecturer in clinical medicine at Glasgow University; but though the children's hospital was not his life's work he was well suited to Garnethill. According to O. H. Mavor he 'was a greater lover of children, and his time at the Sick Children's Hospital was a happy time'.

MacKenzie Anderson was a patient, kindly, infinitely courteous man – a perfect gentleman, people called him. Bitter words were never heard from him, or about him. Mavor thought him 'modest, perhaps to a fault' and said that he had a habit of deferring to the opinions of even the youngest and most ignorant of his colleagues. He was a good listener, though not a fluent talker. 'Nothing human was without interest for him,' noted Mavor. 'When a party of men broke up, it was impossible to say how much or how little he had contributed to the discussion. What was certain was the curious air of benediction that his presence brought. The most unamiable persons felt some warmth towards their neighbours and the most diffident felt themselves to be of some account.'

★   ★   ★

There were new faces in the boardroom too at the turn of the century. Thomas Carlile, the unfussy philanthropist from Paisley, had been succeeded by a series of short-term chairmen; but Charles K. Aitken, who was elected chairman in 1909, was to remain in office for more than 20 years. Andrew Macgeorge, the hospital's first secretary, had died in 1891 but his firm of Macgeorge, Cowan, and Fraser – changing its name to Cowan and Fraser, then to Cowan, Fraser, and

Clapperton, and finally in 1896 to Cowan, Clapperton, and Barclay – remained closely associated with the hospital. Macgeorge's partner, H. H. Galloway, the hospital's first honorary treasurer, was succeeded in 1886 by his colleague M. P. Fraser (later Sir Matthew). After 1891 Fraser combined the offices of secretary and treasurer, and when he left to go to the Scottish Bar in 1895 was succeeded by Alan E. Clapperton. And in 1900 a young solicitor, Robert F. Barclay, who had recently been made a partner in the firm, took over as honorary secretary, Clapperton continuing as treasurer.

These were significant changes for the hospital. Aitken, Barclay, and Clapperton were to remain in office for many years; and Barclay – who first as secretary and later as chairman was to remain associated with the hospital until 1946 – was more than any other man the moving force behind the transfer of the hospital from Garnethill to its new site on Yorkhill.

Chapter 11

THE GREEN SLOPES OF YORKHILL

By the beginning of the century it had become obvious that the hospital was outgrowing its Garnethill home. 'Now every available space is occupied, and further extension on the present site is impossible, even if it were desirable, which for many reasons it is not,' stated the directors. Tenements surrounded the hospital, restricting sunshine and air space; the veterinary college next door in Buccleuch Street was not considered an ideal neighbour for a children's hospital, and unsavoury smells wafting from the stables of the one building into the wards of the other resulted in a feud between the respective directors. Internally the hospital was now out of date – 'the wards, nurses' and doctors' accommodation, servants' quarters, kitchen, laundries, are all closely packed together; patients, nurses, doctors, and servants are living practically in one house and breathing the same air.' Sir Donald MacAlister, Principal of Glasgow University and a patron of the hospital – and himself a distinguished member of the medical profession – went as far as to describe the situation as 'not in the strictest sense hygienic'.

A tiny hospital based on two ordinary dwelling houses, and containing only 74 cots, could hardly hope to cater for an area with a population of two million; even less could it serve, as it attempted to do, the whole of the west of Scotland from the Solway to the Hebrides. Extra cots were placed in the wards – 'which but for the necessity of the case is not desirable' – but still the waiting list grew. In 1901 Kennedy Dalziel and R. H. Parry had enough patients on their books to fill their two wards twice over the next day – but there was no hope of admitting them within two months. By 1907 between

100 and 200 patients were always waiting. 'Many cases for whom hospital treatment was probably their only chance were refused admission because the treatment of their case would take too long,' said Kennedy Dalziel. 'In order that the greatest good be done to the greatest number all the available cots were required for acute cases that could be quickly and certainly cured.' Particularly hard-hit in this respect were those suffering from tubercular disease of the hip joint and the spine, both of which killed or crippled hundreds of Glasgow children every year. Turned away from Garnethill these children were often then rejected also by the overcrowded general hospital – 'surgical outcasts,' Sir Hector Cameron, honorary vice-president of the hospital, called them.

Short-term patients were affected too. Many serious cases which would otherwise have received hospital treatment were operated on at the dispensary, then wrapped in a shawl or blanket and carried home. For Cowcaddens people at least, this was better than carrying the children home across half the city from the out-patient department of a general hospital – a practice described by Sir Hector as 'the surgery of the battlefield'.

Sometimes there were complaints from the family doctors of children who had been turned away, and from the subscribers who had written their lines. Once it was even alleged, on behalf of a child who had been refused admission, that patients were being kept in hospital longer than necessary so that they would not miss the Christmas treat. (Other complaints received by the Garnethill directors included, incidentally, one from a father who claimed that his infant, while in hospital, had been allowed to consume 'considerable quantities of cotton wool'.)

Envious comparisons were made between Glasgow and cities like New York, which had three children's hospitals with a total of 750 beds; and it was noted that Edinburgh and Aberdeen, although smaller than Glasgow, had more beds in their children's hospitals.

'The King and his poorest subjects are on equality when it comes to sickness,' said Sir Hector Cameron, summing up the situation with his customary eloquence. In medical charity it was, he said, 'a perfect mockery' to talk of giving less than the best – and many children, such as those who had to be hived off from the hospital to the dispensary, were not receiving the best possible but only the best available.

Or as George Middleton put it, in more homely terms, the hospital was passing out of its boyhood, and like all boys it had outgrown its clothes and needed a new suit.

There had been talk of a new hospital in 1902, when Kennedy Dalziel had received 'some indication' that Sir Thomas Lipton, the King's grocer, might be willing to assist financially in the building. But the directors, in view of their financial position and the expenditure on the new country branch, were unwilling to commit themselves to a definite scheme before Lipton had committed himself to supporting it; and Lipton may have seen things the other way round, for the idea came to nothing.

But with the waiting list growing month by month matters could not be postponed indefinitely, and the first formal step towards a new hospital was taken in 1907. Years later, at the hospital's jubilee in 1932, Principal Robert Rait of Glasgow University was to look back on that year of 1907 as the most crucial in the hospital's history.

Early in the year, with privately canvassed subscriptions amounting to £27,000, the directors launched a public appeal for £100,000 – the signatories included Lord Kelvin. The appeal was launched at a 'drawing room meeting' convened by the Lord Provost, Sir William Bilsland, in the banqueting hall of the City Chambers. Hector Cameron was in characteristically good voice, and in the course of his lengthy speech described the hospital as being 'at a very grave crisis' in its history.

A reproduction of 'Only This Little One', by Charles E. Stewart, was used in the appeal – and years later, in 1952, the hospital received a gift of the original painting. Poetry also played its part. Backing the appeal were reprints of a poignant poem, *The Little Brick Builders*, by one Robert Bird. The poem had been published by *The Glasgow News* in 1907 when it opened 'The People's Fund' to raise £10,000 in small amounts for the new hospital. A shortened version runs:

> Come a' ye rosy cheekit weans!
> Wha splash through dubs and loup ower stanes,
> Lay doun your barrows, whups, and reins,
>   Your preens and pirns,
> And hear aboot the griefs and pains,
>   O' some puir bairns.

The laughin' moon, frae her blue height,
Keeks not upon a sweeter sight,
Than sleepin' weans, kissed for the night,
    On brow and e'e,
Sent skimming aff, on bowsters white,
    Ower dreamland's sea.

But, there are ither bairns as sweet,
Wha scarce can lift their little feet:
In hopeless plight, they sit and greet,
    And cry in vain
For some cool hand to cool their heat,
    And soothe their pain.

My bonny rosebud! are ye willing,
A modest bairnie's part fulfilling –
To beg for love? your wee heart thrilling,
    To help the sick –
Well pleased that ilka guid white shilling
    Should build a brick!

Everyone, of course, had his own ideas about what the new hospital should be like. James Finlayson wanted it to concentrate on medical rather than surgical cases. James Nicoll wanted it to include accommodation for nursing mothers. Kennedy Dalziel, and many others, wanted it to provide for many more babies – a suggestion which was in fact carried out. Lord Blythswood, a patron of the hospital, wished the patients to be housed in 'inexpensive temporary erections' since he believed that after buildings had served as hospitals for a considerable time they should be got rid of altogether – they might well, he added starkly, be burned down.

Suggestions that the hospital should be built in the country were dismissed quickly and conclusively, on the grounds of inconvenience to both patients and doctors (at one annual meeting Hector Cameron asked if anyone present would think of boarding the first express train if his child suddenly became gravely ill). It was also considered important that the hospital should be within easy reach of the university, so that it could become a teaching centre. Other requirements included a site 'where the maximum of sunshine and fresh air will be obtained'; a building large enough to receive the cases sent from the dispensary as well as from other sources; and accommodation for a nursing staff large enough to enable many very young children to be treated.

For a time it looked as if the new hospital might be built on the grounds of the university observatory in Dowanhill. Sketch plans were actually drawn up, but the idea was abandoned 'on account of the inadequacy of the available ground, the exorbitant price asked by the owners – the University – and difficulties as to drainage and water supply'. (The price asked was £15,000.)

John James Burnet, the architect of the Western Infirmary, and Dr Donald J. Mackintosh of the Western – 'whose experience in the requirements and construction of hospitals is second to none' – were then asked to report on the three best sites available. The sites which they selected – one was West Balgray House, Kelvinside – were repeatedly visited and studied 'in all conditions of wind and weather'; the medical chiefs were asked for their opinions; and it was 'the unanimous view of all consulted that a portion of the lands of Yorkhill had most to commend it of all the sites which it was within the power of the directors to obtain'.

An 19-acre site containing 'the best and highest parts of the lands of Yorkhill' was bought for £16,000. The purchasers were highly pleased with the ground's 'openness, airiness, and elevation, its accessibility from all parts of the city by road, rail, tramway, subway, and ferry and its proximity to the university'. Standing high above the river Clyde the hospital, it was noted, would 'not be affected by noise or smoke more than any city hospital must be'. To the west the hospital would look across to the Western Infirmary and Glasgow University; and the university, it seemed, looked back – the Principal, Sir Donald MacAlister, said he saw the green slopes of Yorkhill from his window every day, and to his eyes it would take on a new beauty when it was crowned with a building – 'whether plain or ornamental it matters not' – dedicated to the succour of sick children. MacAlister had himself once been in charge of the children's wards at Addenbrooke's Hospital in Cambridge.

High on the green slopes stood Yorkhill House, which was demolished during the construction of the hospital. Overlooking a picturesque landscape, the house had a romantic history. It was built in 1805 by a wealthy merchant and acquired eight years later by Andrew Gilbert, a Glasgow underwriter. Gilbert's niece had her portrait painted by a young artist, John Graham, who was later to become a leading portrait painter; later the two married and lived in Yorkhill House, and under the terms of Gilbert's will the artist adopted his father-in-law's name and became John Graham-Gilbert. Lord Kelvin once sat for Graham-Gilbert, whose best-known works include his portrait of Mrs Isabella Craigie Campbell, now in Glasgow Art Gallery. The house remained in the family after the artist's death. Garnethill's very first annual report records a £50 donation from 'C. A. Crerar Gilbert, Yorkhill'. The last occupant,

Yorkhill House – demolished to make way for the construction of the hospital.

Mrs Crerar Gilbert, lived there until shortly before the hospital acquired the site; and the gardens and vineries had been, it was noted, 'kept up suitably.'

This was only the topmost layer of Yorkhill's long history – though the name itself was comparatively recent. In 1868 workmen trenching ground on the summit of the hill turned up an assortment of Roman coins, bronze finger rings, and fragments of Samian pottery. This was almost the first trace of Roman occupation found in Glasgow, and it was conjectured that Yorkhill was once occupied by a small fort held perhaps by a centurion's guard drafted from the garrison in one of the large camps, and probably later made obsolete by the building of the Antonine Wall.

It was only by a hair-breadth margin that the hospital was not scooped by Glasgow Corporation in the acquisition of the site. In 1906 the corporation had considered purchasing it, and the proposal was defeated only by the casting vote of the Lord Provost – who had in fact backed the project but in view of the division of opinion was unwilling to use his vote to tip the scales in its favour. (Later, in 1920, the corporation bought four acres of vacant land to the south of the hospital, and to this the directors added five acres of their own grounds 'on condition that the Corporation lay out both plots as a public park or pleasure ground and maintain them as such, open and unbuilt on, in all time coming'.)

★   ★   ★

Among many city architects who wrote to the directors asking to be considered for the Yorkhill commission was Charles Rennie Mackintosh's firm – Honeyman, Keppie, and Mackintosh. But an *art nouveau* sick children's hospital was not to be; the services of John James Burnet, who had advised in the selection of the site, were retained, and also those of Donald Mackintosh as consultant.

The Burnets, father and son, were a remarkable architectural family who made significant alterations to the face of Glasgow. John Burnet senior had designed the Clydesdale Bank in St Vincent Place, and Cleveden Terrace. His son, sent to study at l'Ecole des Beaux Arts in Paris, returned to his native city to design, among an imposing variety of buildings, Charing Cross Mansions and the Academy of Music as well as the Western Infirmary. It has been said of him that in addition to his important contributions to commercial architecture he 'laid the foundation for the modern advance that has revolutionised hospital design'.

After being selected as architect for the extension to the British Museum, Burnet had opened a London office in 1905; but on his regular visits to Glasgow he personally supervised the Yorkhill designs. Mr Alfred Lochhead, the Glasgow architect, who was a junior draughtsman in the firm's Glasgow office during the commission – 'the work was never known to us as anything but "the Sick Kids" ' – recalls Burnet's perfectionist approach to the task. 'Nothing but the best would do for Burnet,' said Mr Lochhead, recalling how the architect would turn up at the Glasgow office and

John James Burnet's building (with later additions).

scrap an entire month's work 'if he thought things could be done just a little bit better'.

The task confronting Burnet at Yorkhill was very different from the one that had faced James Sellars 30 years before on Garnethill. Yorkhill was to be the largest children's hospital in the kingdom, with the exception of Great Ormond Street in London; and whereas Sellars and James Whitelaw had plodded round children's hospitals in England, Burnet and Donald Mackintosh gathered ideas and information on visits to America, France, and, above all, Germany.

In line with the latest ideas of hospital construction the pavilion system was adopted, with widely spaced ward blocks linked by broad corridors. This ensured the maximum light, sunshine, and fresh air, and for the same reason the blocks had a north-south alignment. Originally it was planned that each block should be only two storeys high, but the cost was found to be prohibitive and the plans were recast to reduce the number of blocks and increase their height.

87

There were 12 wards and two operating theatres. In contrast with Garnethill and its painted windows, Yorkhill's wards had large windows with low sills 'so that the children could see out'. At the outer ends of the wards the windows opened on to large verandahs, where children could be wheeled in their cots: tubercular patients spent much of the winter there, and on summer days visiting mothers and grannies sat knitting in the sunshine (latterly the verandahs were enclosed with glass to provide playrooms). The children could also be taken by elevator to the flat roofs of the wards, where shelters were built.

The design, materials, and finish were of the simplest – 'No money has been spent on elaborations of moulded or carved work.' The hospital was built of brick, and some critics thought it looked too severe. 'But', retorted the directors, 'the strong, direct lines of each block, the general colour scheme, the light colour of the glazed connecting corridors and airing verandahs, and the uniformity of level of the flat roofs, result in a whole which is dignified and pleasing.' Not everyone was convinced. James Cowan, author of *From Glasgow's Treasure Chest*, a collection of snippets of the city's history,

The frontage of J. J. Burnet's building at Yorkhill.

was later to refer to 'the useful, but unsightly masses of the Royal Hospital for Sick Children'.

But not even the critics could have denied that the hospital had its splendours – the entrance hall and boardroom in panelled oak, the large conservatory with a fountain at one end. The conservatory was always 'laden with sweet-smelling plants and ferns' – and it wasn't long before someone presented the hospital with goldfish for the fountain basin. Near the fountain rested the statue of a baby, which touched the hearts of *The Nursing and Midwives' Journal*. 'This delicately wrought little figure', reported the journal, 'lies on its side in the peaceful, confident sleep of the healthy, happy infant.' The hospital's housemen took a less sentimental view, and the baby was destined to find itself abandoned more than once on the doorstep of the medical superintendent's home.

The cost of the hospital was more than 10 times that of its predecessor on Garnethill – about £140,000 including site, building, and equipment. At the opening in 1914 it was announced that this sum had been fully raised. The money came both from individuals and from institutions, and some of it had been raised at special events. Boy Scouts who had been given temporary use of the grounds held a field day for the benefit of the hospital, and a garden fête was held at a stately home near Cardross, with tea on the croquet lawn and a 'rustic model cottage' on the tennis court.

The launching of the public appeal in 1907 had been followed by a general improvement in the hospital's financial situation, and it was noted in 1909 that 'the surplus has been the largest and the finances most flourishing on each occasion when the institution has been brought most prominently before the public'. Nevertheless it was thought wise to limit the number of beds at first to 200, on the grounds that the pavilion system would allow relatively easy and inexpensive additions at a later date.

From first to last the hospital board had given a close personal supervision to the building. There was an expedition of directors to Bothwell Park brickworks to inspect a sample wall of the proposed bricks, and to Stobhill Hospital, which had been built with them; and Robert Barclay, the honorary secretary, is said hardly to have left the site while the building was going up. What the board and John James Burnet did not and could not see was that the cement – lightweight and typical of its time – was not adhering firmly to certain of the steel beams, that some of those beams were vulnerable to corrosion, and that half a century later the building would be declared in a state of 'potential avalanche'. 'It was something that could not possibly have been foreseen,' as Mr Lochhead points out.

Meanwhile, life in the crowded wards of Scott Street went on as usual, with its ups and downs and its minor upheavals as well as its major dramas. Master Solomon Lazarus hurt himself falling out of his cot. The Governor of Duke Street Prison complained that his niece, a nurse, had been unfairly treated by the matron (the charge was declared unfounded). The residents were reprimanded for being late for work, and the directors took to dropping in on the hospital early in the morning to check up on them. And the matron, Miss Julia Simpson, who succeeded Mrs Harbin in 1903, found herself briefly in the limelight. *The Glasgow News* published a photograph of Miss Simpson, plump, comely-looking, and in the company of 'one of her temporary charges' – a baby lion. The lion cub was one of several brought in – from, the *News* said, 'the jungle' – for the entertainment of the children.

But as John James Burnet's building went up brick by brick on Yorkhill, attention became increasingly focussed on the future. Glasgow had been slow off the mark in providing for sick children; but soon it was to lead the field.

Chapter 12

A STATE OCCASION

ON the afternoon of July 7, 1914, in the brilliant sunshine typical of those weeks before the outbreak of war, the new hospital was opened by King George V and Queen Mary.

The King and Queen were then on a State visit to Scotland – they opened the re-built Royal Infirmary on the same day – and no part of it can have been more stately than that afternoon at Yorkhill. 'Picturesque to a degree' was *The Evening Citizen*'s description of the scene. *The Glasgow Herald* found it 'peculiarly exhilarating as a spectacle'.

A temporary royal pavilion, 'dignified in its lines and chaste in its decorative scheme,' had been set up outside the main doorway. A canopy of white muslin covered the pavilion, crimson carpets 'made a striking contrast', and Dorothy Perkins roses were arrayed round the supporting pillars. In the centre of the pavilion a pair of seventeenth-century Scottish high-backed armchairs, covered in red velvet, had been provided for the King and Queen (one of the chairs was to be used again half a century later at the opening of the Queen Mother's Hospital next door). The marshalling of Boy Scouts and members of the Boys' Brigade, and the music of bands, 'beguiled the time of waiting.'

A crowd of nearly 10,000 had assembled. 'Friends of the hospital from all parts of the country, from London to Skye' waited on the grandstands flanking the pavilion. A 'large contingent' of the workers who had built the hospital watched from a stand of their own. Scouts and Guides stood shoulder to shoulder along the royal route round the hospital grounds.

The Boys' Brigade had provided no fewer than three bands, as well as buglers on the east and west towers who sounded the alert on the approach of the cavalcade. Preceded by outriders, flanked by mounted staff officers, and escorted by officers of the Royal Scots Greys bearing the royal standard, the King and Queen and Princess Mary travelled in a carriage drawn by four bays. On their arrival a Royal Scots Greys trumpeter sounded the salute, the royal standard was hoisted on the pavilion flagstaff, and the Lord Provost conducted the royal party to their regal seats. After the exchange of written addresses with the honorary president (the Duke of Montrose) the King was asked to accept an ornamental silver key, and to unlock the main doors of the new hospital. Then: 'The King proceeded up the few steps and, having opened the doors, turned, and, facing the large assembly, all standing, said in a clear voice, "I have much pleasure in declaring this hospital open," the words being received with loud cheers.'

There followed a royal tour of inspection of the still empty hospital, the King being accompanied by Charles Aitken, chairman of the directors, and the Queen by Robert Barclay, director and honorary secretary. Before entering Ward 9 the Queen was invited by Robert Barclay to name it the 'King George V and Queen Mary Ward',

John Burnet's building before the official opening in 1914, with the royal pavilion under construction in preparation for the ceremony.

The royal party arriving at Yorkhill for the official opening in 1914.

which she did by unveiling a plaque above the door with the royal arms quartered in the Scottish fashion. From the balcony at the top of the west staircase the King and Queen, gazing out over the serried ranks of Scouts and Guides, admired the view of the Renfrewshire hills. In the conservatory they were received by doctors ranged on one side and nurses on the other, the Queen singling out the matron, Miss Julia Simpson, to 'ask several questions regarding the nursing staff'. In the theatres they expressed interest in the way the search-light principle had been adapted to illuminate the operating tables. 'Ah, the searchlight – you have scored with that,' said the King to Kennedy Dalziel.

The tour of inspection over, the royal carriage drew off 'amidst ringing cheers and the strains of the national anthem' – and the hospital was thrown open to the inspection of ticket-holders.

★   ★   ★

Somewhat less ceremonious was the actual transfer, two months later, from 45 Scott Street to the spacious splendours of the new

93

hospital – and it is recorded that 'not a few felt a certain regret when the time finally came to leave old hospital'.

But at least the old building was still to serve the interests of youth, and has done so ever since. It was bought by 'a body of charitable ladies and gentlemen' for use as a girls' hostel. But Germany was on the march, and before being put to this purpose it served briefly as a home for Belgian refugees.

Crowded scene at the royal opening ceremony in July 1914.

Today, as the annexe of Garnethill Convent School, it still bears many traces of its past life – the bas relief of mother and child above the door, the rich stained glass windows on the stairway, the cupola window above the old post-mortem room, the sculptured palm branches and crown of thorns on the mortuary door. Nursery rhymes no longer adorn the windows, but children's paintings hang on the walls of the old top-floor ward. On the flat roof of what was once the Carlile ward classes have sometimes been held on summer days, and the glass shelter which protected sickly children from the wind remained till the early 1950s. The pupils themselves are aware of Scott Street's past, and have also delved deeply into the history of the dispensary. Their teachers belong to the Sisters of Mercy, the order that assisted Florence Nightingale in the Crimean War.

Chapter 13

MILITARY OCCUPATION

'A hospital is like a battleship,' declared Sir Hector Cameron at the annual meeting in 1915. 'It is at its best when newly launched.' The simile was, unfortunately, apt in a more obvious sense. Four weeks after the opening ceremony war was declared, later some of the wards were occupied by wounded officers, and the hospital was not to function at full strength till well after 1918.

'Yorkhill War Hospital, formerly known as the Royal Hospital for Sick Children' was the somewhat peremptory wording of a Scottish Command order of 1915. However Yorkhill was not entirely taken over by the military authorities – four wards only were requisitioned. The hospital was told at short notice to prepare these wards for adult occupants, and the directors were obliged to point out that since Yorkhill was designed for children under 13 'it would be necessary to purchase beds, mattresses, blankets, linen, crockery, and other equipment for adults, and also to make sundry alterations in the equipment of and even possibly structural alterations to the existing lavatory accommodation'.

Army and naval officers, both British and Colonial, occupied the military wards. Had doctors attending the occupants of Ward 10 but known it, they were treating one of the hospital's future chiefs; one of the patients was a young officer called Matthew White – who in later years was to rule over that same ward as senior surgeon to the children's hospital.

Technically these wards were a branch of the major military hospital at Stobhill, and the cost was met by the Government and by voluntary donations. The patients were treated by military doctors (mainly those already on the hospital staff), and by military nurses under the direction of a military Sister. Captain Gracie, a Partick doctor, was appointed medical officer in charge of the military wards.

For the hospital authorities the military years were not happy ones. 'The commandeering of the four wards was a mistake,' stated the directors in one of their letters to the Scottish Command. Captain Gracie, too, appears to have had his moments of frustration. The board minutes record the captain's request for the use of a typewriter, and tersely add: 'The directors agreed not to grant the request.'

There were also less trifling tiffs with the military authorities – for example, over lapses in the military payments for the officers' food. Once the directors were driven to despatch a telegram to the War Office announcing that in view of the fact that no funds had been received responsibility for feeding the officers would pass to the War Office on the following Monday. A cheque arrived quickly.

Alarm, despondency, and indignation were felt in 1917 when the following abrupt letter was received from the Scottish Command:

'As more accommodation is required in the Command for sick officers is it possible please for your Board to hand over the whole of the Royal Hospital for Sick Children to the Military Authorities?'

The directors replied that it certainly was not possible. They neatly pin-pointed the absurdity of the situation by observing that the general hospitals 'existed for the treatment of the very adults who meantime have been transferred to and form part of the military forces'. The proposal came to nothing.

The military occupation of the dispensary was much briefer. One day soldiers from Maryhill Barracks were marched down to West Graham Street – and after a short interval marched back to Maryhill minus their tonsils.

As a military hospital Yorkhill was entitled to immediate official notice by telephone of impending air raids – in advance of the public warning. On May 2, 1916, advance warning was received of a Zeppelin raid. The children were hastily removed to the basement – so hastily that time was not taken to label the patients, and after the klaxons had sounded the all-clear some of them had to be rediagnosed. After this false alarm it was decided that in future patients who were seriously ill should not be taken from the wards till the last moment –

'there always being a possibility that the Zeppelins would not actually reach the city.' The age of the four-minute warning was still mercifully far in the future.

The military requisitioning of the four wards put great pressure on the remaining part of the hospital, and soon Yorkhill was experiencing the old, familiar Garnethill problems of overcrowded wards and long waiting lists. The staff, too, were under considerable strain. Many doctors and nurses were away on military service, and the physicians and surgeons who remained behind found themselves doing at least double duty. At the dispensary two instead of four doctors treated between 150 and 200 children daily – and, as was pointed out, 'it is no light forenoon's work for one man to examine and prescribe for 80 children.' Final-year medical students were brought in as hospital residents, and a layman was put in charge of the X-rays.

The strains and tensions of wartime conditions may have had something to do with the sudden resignation of the matron, Miss Julia Simpson, who had earlier played an important part in the transfer of work from Garnethill to the new hospital. The hospital's house committee had complained about certain aspects of the nursing, and some sort of disagreement appears to have broken out about the right of doctors to make their complaints to the board rather than to the matron herself. The lines of the argument are unclear, but the upshot was that Miss Simpson, in spite of an attempt by the directors to dissuade her, submitted her resignation in 1916. This was followed by a petition from 59 nurses who wished the directors to ask Miss Simpson to reconsider her decision – which they declined to do, on the grounds that she had already been given ample opportunity.

Wartime conditions were also reflected in the reports of the hospital's almoner, who had been appointed in 1915 to follow up cases in the homes of patients. There was, for example, the case of 'K.K.':

'A girl of 4 years – suffering from nephritis, the motherless child of a soldier, lived with her grandmother. The house was miserably poor, dark, and dirty. Grandmother, too old to look after child properly, at first refused to consent to have K.K. sent to a home. Case reported to Govan Parish with a view to having pressure brought to bear upon the grandmother, who finally consented to have the child sent to a Roman Catholic home. K.K. taken to The Orphanage, Rothesay, where she will remain till her father returns from the war.'

November 11, 1918, had been marked down in the directors' diaries as the day of a board meeting. When the time came and they assembled in the boardroom the chairman, Charles Aitken, 'made a few suitable remarks on the good news just received that an armistice with Germany had been signed.' The following summer there was a special excursion for nurses in celebration of the peace; and at an entertainment given for the children each one received from Glasgow Corporation a medal, a bag of buns, and a bar of cream chocolate.

At Yorkhill, as in other places, there was no immediate return to normality after the armistice. The military evacuation was not completed till late in 1919; and because of the 'protracted delays of the military authorities' in settling for damage done to the wards, together with the hospital's poor financial situation – income for 1919 fell short of expenditure by £10,000 – it was not until the end of 1921 that all four requisitioned wards were put to their originally intended use.

At last, more than seven years after the official opening, Yorkhill was poised to fulfil its considerable potential.

Chapter 14

YORKHILL AND GILMOREHILL

'On a winter evening one can stand in one of the upper wards and looking out of the windows see on one side the motley traffic faring into the waterways of the world, and from another across roofs and chimneys and gallant city shrubberies to the low line of hills that screen Glasgow to the north-west, and which at the end of a December day are steeped rose and purple in the fading sunlight.' So wrote a visitor to Yorkhill in the 1920s. And the hospital's imposing situation was soon matched by its new eminence in the world of paediatric medicine.

Yorkhill meant more than just a bigger and better building; it lifted the hospital into quite a different league. Two developments in particular transformed its character – the reorganisation of the visiting staff and the forging of a special relationship with Glasgow University.

When the children's hospital moved to Yorkhill it was decided that the honorary staff should visit the wards every day and should not hold visiting posts at other hospitals. This meant the resignation of Kennedy Dalziel and James Nicoll (who, however, remained associated with the hospital as honorary consultants) and of many others whose major hospital work was elsewhere. But it paved the way for the coming of the paediatrician. Admittedly, with only a small honorarium being offered until the late 1930s – later for the surgeons – there was no great material incentive to graduates to enter the field. 'I well remember,' writes Professor James Hutchison, the present occupant of the Chair of Child Health at Glasgow University, 'on deciding to embark on a paediatric career in 1937,

A ward verandah in the 1920s.

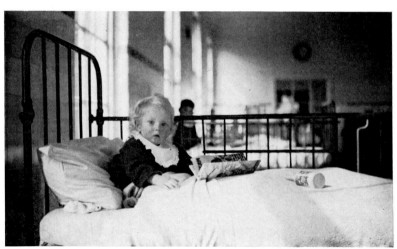

A patient at the country branch in the 1930s.

being taken aside by a successful if worldly physician of this city and asked if I were mad.' John Thomson of Edinburgh, known as the father of Scottish paediatrics, once remarked that at least the limited earnings of paediatricians ensured that they would be spared the jealousies bedevilling their colleagues.

On its new and more westerly site, and with its up-to-date design and equipment, the hospital was well placed to forge links with Glasgow University. In 1914 it had become compulsory – hitherto it had only been recommended – for medical students to receive lectures and clinical instruction in the medical and surgical diseases of childhood. Organised teaching was postponed by the war but was put into practice afterwards, and a scheme of post-graduate study was also introduced at the hospital. Now, too, in the post-war years came the swift development of university lectureships linked with the hospital. First Leonard Gow, a Glasgow shipowner, gave £5000 to found a university lectureship in the diseases of infancy and childhood, in memory of his father; and Robert Barclay, secretary of the hospital, gave the same amount to found a lectureship in paediatric surgery and orthopaedics. A condition of both the Gow and the Barclay lectureships, which were chiefly clinical, was that they should be associated with the hospital – the lecturers being a visiting physician and a visiting surgeon with wards at Yorkhill. It was also stipulated that the physician should have a consultative connection with the Royal Maternity Hospital; and the same practice was soon adopted for the surgical lectureship.

A few years later, in 1924, came the founding of a university chair associated with the hospital. The Samson Gemmell Chair of Medical Paediatrics, in memory of the physician who had been so closely associated with the hospital in its Garnethill days, was established with £20,000 bequeathed by his brother. Then, 'with a view to completing the team of scientific workers,' Principal Donald MacAlister arranged for the appointment of a university lecturer in biochemistry in relation to infancy and childhood who would also be Yorkhill's biochemist and work in the hospital laboratory. In 1928 the Gardiner research lectureship in the pathology of the diseases of childhood and infancy was established, also in association with the hospital. (From 1930 doctors teaching students at the hospital were recognised as honorary lecturers at the university.)

All this set the scene for the development of Yorkhill as a major teaching and research centre, thus fulfilling the hopes of the hospital's Victorian founders. The hospital had a team of scientific workers associated with the university which no other children's hospital in the country could boast. The Samson Gemmell Chair of Medical Paediatrics (now the Chair of Child Health) was the first of its kind in Britain and made Glasgow into the only academic paediatric centre in the country in the 1920s (although Birmingham was to forge ahead in the next decade). Even in the United States and on the Continent the coming of the fully fledged paediatrician had resulted more in the clinical description of diseases than in major research. So important was Glasgow's position that by the early 1930s the story was being told of a young London doctor who travelled to Berlin to make a special study of some children's disease; the professor there expressed surprise that he had travelled so far and inquired, 'why did you not go to Glasgow?'

★   ★   ★

'A hospital set on a hill should not be hid,' remarked Principal Sir Donald MacAlister after a large and cosmopolitan reception had been given at Yorkhill when the British Medical Association held their annual meeting in Glasgow in 1922. The visitors had expressed 'admiration, not unmixed with a touch of envy'.

There was a cosmopolitan touch, too, about some of the royal visits to Yorkhill. The Prince and Princess of Siam turned up in 1922 and 'expressed themselves as highly delighted with what they had seen'.

Princess Mary appeared on the scene in the following year – and shared the limelight with a small patient. *The Daily Record* reported:

'Princess Mary met another Princess at the Royal Hospital for Sick Children. This was little "Princess Helen", otherwise Helen Lafferty, who lives at Cleland, Lanarkshire, and who presented Her Royal Highness with a bouquet. Nobody seems to know exactly how Helen got her title, but ever since she came into the Hospital, some weeks ago, she has thus described herself.'

In 1927 the King and Queen opened the new Kelvin Hall, the exhibition hall built opposite the Art Galleries to replace a smaller one of the same name burned down two years before. On the initiative of the Yorkhill directors the royal party was welcomed by a

Princess Mary visits Yorkhill. On the left are Campbell Suttie, the medical superintendent, and Mary Cameron, the matron.

Awaiting the royal procession to the Kelvin Hall in 1927.

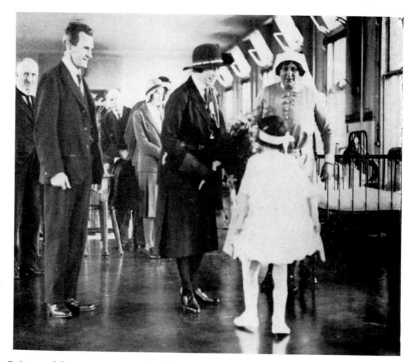

Princess Mary meets a patient in 1930. Also in the foreground are Alexander MacLennan and the matron, Mary Cameron.

great muster of youth organisations on the slopes fronting the hospital and facing the rear entrance of the hall. After various false alarms in which lorries and laundry vans were enthusiastically hailed, the 5000 young people in assorted uniforms 'gave full vent to their lung power in a rendering of the national anthem' as the royal visitors arrived. A group of patients on one of the hospital balconies joined in the cheering, and a reporter noted that 'the nurses and maids of the hospital, in their spotless caps and aprons, formed a very pretty background to the army of youngsters'.

There was, in contrast, a solo performance by one of the patients when Princess Mary, dressed in what one newspaper described as 'her magnificent Guide uniform', made another visit to the hospital in 1930. The hero of the hour was a small boy who had lost his sight in an accident. As *The Bulletin* reported: 'Sitting up in his little scarlet bed jacket, his head swathed in bandages, the blind child sang the rollicking ditty, "Sailing up the Clyde." '

There were cheerful scenes in the wards, too, during the annual Christmas treats. Friends and supporters of the hospital were invited to look in on these occasions; and *The Glasgow Herald*, which reported this event annually, gave the following exuberant description of the scene witnessed by visitors on Christmas Eve, 1924:

'Passing through the conservatory, where in a setting of palms a fountain splashed refreshing showers on the coloured fish disporting themselves in the great basin, the visitors found their way into the several wards. These, always spotless and bright and airy, were for this day glimpses of fairyland. Coloured lights tempered the restful shade, and looming up in the shimmering silver and green, a great Christmas tree stood in the middle of each ward. From these toys were being taken and distributed among the wide-eyed, happy children in the cots. It was a sight to bring the lump to the throat in the almost-pain of emotion to see tiny tots hugging dolls and brave little lads tootling on trumpets, or older ones lying surrounded by books, a happy smile on their faces. Through the ward came a little miss riding in a coach "drawn" by a prancing wooden steed, whose prancing, nevertheless, was guided by a careful nurse.'

In among such moments of jollification came the customary domestic crises. During the coal strike of 1921 the supply of boiler coal nearly ran out, and 26 tons were borrowed from the university 'with the kind consent of Principal MacAlister'. Three years later the hospital was afflicted by what the medical superintendent described as a plague of cockroaches; but these were somewhat more easily stamped out than the annual crop of bogus collectors who masqueraded as representatives of the hospital and brandished copies of the annual report to add a note of authenticity to their cause.

On the brighter side, it was decreed in 1925 that instead of having butter only once a week and margarine on other days, patients should have butter every day.

★   ★   ★

The hospital's finances did not greatly flourish in the first few years after the war. Naturally it had been realised from the beginning that the new hospital would be much more expensive to maintain than the old one. What hadn't been bargained for was the war, when charity was diverted to military causes, together with the post-war rise in prices. Between 1915 and 1920 the hospital's annual expenditure on food rose from £3700 to £7700; on milk, from £850 to £2230; and on medical and surgical appliances, from £700 to £4400. The wages bill doubled.

Fortunately subscriptions also increased – especially contributions from employees in factories and warehouses, which were made more systematic in those years. But this was not sufficient to offset the sharp price rises of 1920; and in that year expenditure alarmingly eroded the hospital's capital. 'When an Institution begins to subsist on its capital the result is as ruinous and the end is as certainly in sight as would be the case in an individual, and that is the position of most of the Hospitals and Infirmaries in Scotland today,' wrote the directors in 1921, in their evidence to the Parliamentary Commission on Hospitals. They argued that voluntary hospitals should be entitled to financial relief in recognition of the public work they undertook.

At the same time, Yorkhill faced considerable extra expenditure. No sooner was the hospital operating at full strength, after the restoration of the military wards, than extensions were urgently needed – more wards, more accommodation for nurses, more research facilities. So in December 1924 a public appeal for £75,000 was launched, with more than half this sum already privately subscribed. 'No cause could be more inspiringly pleaded to all classes, rich and poor alike, without regard to sex or sect,' commented *The Glasgow Herald* in a leader. 'The wisest of men, the greatest of poets could not plead so powerfully as those tiny voices from the wards at Yorkhill.' The launching of the fund was followed by a radio broadcast by Robert Barclay – one of the very first such appeals to be broadcast from the Scottish Studio of the B.B.C. (5 SC), which had opened in Bath Street in 1923.

The public appeal was to be illustrated by the picture of a child, and heated debate arose as to whether it would be psychologically better to show a pale and wan child or a healthy chubby one. The picture eventually chosen, showing a healthy, curly-haired little boy in striped trousers, was a photograph taken by the honorary secretary, Robert Barclay, of one of his sons, the younger brother of the present chairman of the board.

The appeal was a great success: all the money was raised within four months. A fortnight after the launching of the appeal visitors

The country branch in the mid-30s.

View of Gilmorehill from Yorkhill in 1927.

arriving for the Christmas treat saw through the December dusk workmen digging the foundations of the new buildings in the miry clay near the main entrance to the hospital. 'As the men toiled,' reported the *Herald*, 'interested glances were cast their way by many representative citizens as they passed in to these noble halls of healing.' Two new wings were built, providing extensions to the nurses' and administrative quarters, and releasing space in the original building for more beds and new departments. At the same

The country branch at Drumchapel after the opening of the extension.

time planning went ahead for, among other things, a new administration block, a re-organised X-ray department, and a bigger pathological department. Not all the hospital's building programme, however, had been carried through by the outbreak of the Second World War.

The country branch was also extended, with the help of £17,000 from the trustees of Peter Coats, of the Paisley thread manufacturers. (The Coats family were consistent and generous supporters of the hospital.) By now Anniesland Boulevard was becoming so built up that there were initial doubts about whether to build the new extensions at Drumchapel or elsewhere. But Drumchapel was decided on, and three main wards – doubling the accommodation – and a nurses' home were added. Much was made of the new 'panel' system of heating, with pipes embedded in the ceiling to prevent the vitiating effects of the radiator system; this was a novelty in hospitals at that time.

When the extensions were officially opened in 1930 the scarlet-jacketed patients of the country branch received their guests with, it was reported, complete equanimity; and 'one small gentleman gravely remarked that he would be glad to renew the acquaintance of a lady visitor when he returned to town'.

Chapter 15

PAEDIATRIC PIONEERING

'A tumult of characters' is one doctor's description of the staff at Yorkhill between the wars. It was an age of medical individualists (not that these have been lacking at Yorkhill at any period), and the hospital witnessed many remarkable scenes – the physician doing his ward rounds in hunting clothes, the surgeon soaring over Yorkhill in his private aeroplane.

Dominant among the tumult of personalities in the 1920s was Leonard Findlay, the first occupant of the Samson Gemmell Chair. Findlay was a remarkable man. He left a lasting mark on the hospital, and on the memories of all who knew him there. 'For sheer, rude enjoyment Leonard Findlay's ward rounds always remain with me as the most stimulating, crazy mornings I have ever spent,' comments Professor Stanley Graham, who later occupied the same Chair. And Dr Mary Stevenson recalls: 'I used to think when he arrived in the morning that an electric shock had gone through the building.'

Findlay, the son of a doctor, was educated at Allan Glen's School and Glasgow University, and early in his career was a houseman at Garnethill, then a physician at the dispensary. Early on he became interested in rickets, and it was natural that he should have been one of the few doctors in the old hospital to remain on the staff when this meant giving up their other hospital work. At Yorkhill he became the first Gow lecturer and, a little later and in logical sequence, the first Samson Gemmell Professor (he had in fact been Gemmell's assistant at the Western). At Yorkhill, with its brand new laboratories, he quickly and efficiently built up a department unique in the country at that time. He and John Thomson of Edinburgh are regarded as the founders of paediatrics in Scotland, and certainly Findlay played an enormous part in putting Yorkhill on the paediatric map. His reputation was international: young graduates of all nationalities – Americans, assorted Europeans, Australians, even a Chinese doctor – were drawn to Yorkhill. Dr A. K. Bowman, later to become senior administrative medical officer of the Western Regional Hospital Board, spent some years in practice in the United States during the time when Findlay was in full cry at Yorkhill, and recalls that 'among the paediatricians whom I met there was universal high regard for Dr Findlay, and it was frequently said that he had raised the status of Yorkhill to that of an international institution'.

Findlay had a magnetic personality and a striking appearance. To his contemporaries he looked old-fashioned, though his sideburns would pass unremarked in 1972. 'He looked, perhaps he liked to look, as though he had just stepped from the frame of a portrait by Raeburn,' wrote the paediatrician Hector Charles Cameron (the son of Sir Hector), who knew Findlay in London. Professor Stanley Graham has given the following vivid account of his appearance:

'He was essentially an Edwardian – tall, spare, well dressed, and very distinguished. His hair was a coppery red, plentiful, and worn rather long: and in an age when most men were clean-shaven, he cultivated side whiskers. With a delightful disregard of prevailing fashion, he wore a starched white collar, such as used to be worn with evening dress at the turn of the century, and a dark tie which went twice round the collar, finishing in a bow in front. A monocle dangled casually from a black cord around his neck. He tried at times to do without the cord but this was never a success. In the more serious business of ward rounds or in reading he always wore horn-rimmed glasses. Although Edwardian in appearance, his general demeanour was Dickensian, with the manners and gestures of a member of the Pickwick Club.'

Findlay was a man of fiery, impetuous temperament and argumentative tendencies. 'His intervention in debate', wrote H. C. Cameron, 'almost always was to dissent or demur, indicated not only by what he said but also by a series of long-drawn-out sounds of disapproval through closed lips and with much dubious shaking of the head.' Frequently, Cameron added, discussions in which

Findlay took part 'would degenerate into a dispute as to what he had said and what he had not said, as to what he had meant and what he had not meant'.

His disputatious instincts slowed his progress round the wards. 'Often,' wrote Professor Graham, 'only one or two patients were seen, for heated arguments arose and the end of the allotted time would find the bed strewn with books and journals, the Sister and nurses trembling, and perhaps tempers near breaking point.' Soon, however, 'the air would clear and his essential kindness would return' – and Findlay would retire to his room for tea, drinking it hastily from his saucer before returning to work.

No one appears to have borne him permanent ill will, and his fiery temper and histrionic outbursts have been put down to a deliberate attempt to stimulate students or drive home a point. Certainly he succeeded in keeping people on their toes. 'Findlay used to give you loads of work,' recalls one of his assistants, 'and when you had done it he would say, "Ah, but look at it this way" – and you had to start all over again.'

It was an age of medical autocrats and individualists, and Leonard Findlay was one of them. 'Very much the Herr Professor,' remembers one doctor. Findlay had in fact studied in Germany; and he returned to the Continent after the First World War as director to the League of Nations Red Cross Society in Geneva. Of post-war Vienna he wrote: 'Nowhere did I see any evidence of the degradation and abject poverty that exists in my own city.' And rickets, he noted, was less common.

In Glasgow infantile rickets was still miserably prevalent. In 1918, when research was being carried out, it was 'only with the greatest difficulty that Sister Elinor could find among the patients at the Dispensary a sufficient number of non-rachitic children to act as control subjects'. From 1908 onwards Findlay had been deeply interested in this subject; and now, at Yorkhill, together with Professor Diarmid Noel Paton, he carried out many investigations into the cause of rickets. After confining dogs indoors, and comparing them with others which were allowed to run about, he concluded that rickets were caused by lack of exercise. Attaching little significance to the fact that the confined dogs had lacked sunlight as well as exercise, Findlay denied the importance of sunshine and diet. Though cod-liver oil had been recognised as a cure for rickets since

1887, long before vitamin D was heard of, Findlay insisted that just because sunshine and cod-liver oil cured rickets it did not follow that their lack was the cause of rickets – 'Cod-liver oil is not a normal constituent of a child's diet,' he said. Finally he had to retract – but at least he had been half right, in showing that confinement indoors was a cause of rickets.

Outside medicine Findlay's interests were wide-ranging. On his Sunday afternoon visits with Dr Stanley Graham to their fellow-paediatrician John Thomson in Edinburgh the talk was rarely of paediatrics but ranged over general topics. Old furniture, pictures, and the theatre were among his interests; and one of his Yorkhill colleagues once spotted him at the theatre, the single escort of some half dozen women – Findlay was obviously giving some of the Sisters a night out.

He was rather a restless man. In 1930, in his early 50s – and disappointed, it seems, at not having been made the director of the entire medical unit at Yorkhill – he suddenly departed for London to become physician at the Queen Elizabeth Hospital for Children. But in London, and later in Oxford, he never seems to have made much of a mark. His best work was done in Glasgow, and his greatest achievement was his dynamic and lasting influence on its school of paediatrics. Of great significance was the fact that he had not confined himself to one-man research; with his early training in laboratory methods at the Western – he had worked in the pathology department under Sir Robert Muir – he realised the importance of combining laboratory work with clinical work, and gathered around him a team of assistants whom he encouraged to make full use of pathological and biochemical methods in the clinical study of the patients. 'He was the first British paediatrician to use biochemical methods routinely in the investigation of disease in children, and the first to integrate clinical paediatrics with the basic sciences,' notes Professor James Hutchison. 'Findlay was indeed a pioneer, and he would probably have received greater recognition for his work on rickets, rheumatic fever, congenital syphilis, and so on, but for his "difficult" personality and the fact that he left Glasgow for London in 1930.'

★   ★   ★

Leonard Findlay

Geoffrey Fleming

Geoffrey B. Fleming followed Findlay first as Gow lecturer and later in the Samson Gemmell Chair, which he occupied from 1930 to 1947. In temperament he was Findlay's opposite: modest, unobtrusive, lacking the picturesque presence of his predecessor.

From Haileybury, where he was a contemporary of Clement Attlee, Fleming had gone on to Cambridge University before beginning his medical studies in Glasgow. He belonged to one of the oldest families in Glasgow and was a burgess of the city, following his forbears through 14 generations in the direct line.

As a man of ample private means (he is said to have chosen his Daimlers for their colour and shape rather than their performance) he considered it unbecoming to accept payment for his professional services – and stealthily he made large financial contributions to Yorkhill.

Though work was hardly a matter of urgent economic necessity Fleming was no dilettante. His pioneer work in metabolism after the

114

First World War won him renown both in this country and in the United States, and many well-known paediatricians visited the hospital to see the apparatus he had designed for his investigations. A major problem at that time was the unexplained failure of certain children to thrive (treatment of these marasmic children had met with little success in the hospital's Garnethill days) and it was not known whether this was due to infection or to metabolic disturbance. In order to calculate the metabolic rate of infants of all ages, Fleming devised a respiratory chamber in which the child was completely enclosed in glass. By this means he was able to demonstrate that the metabolic rate of marasmic infants was much lower than that of the healthy child.

Though he lacked the fire and fury of Leonard Findlay, Fleming had his colourful moments. An enthusiastic member of the Lanark and Renfrewshire Hunt – though his unorthodox methods sometimes dismayed his fellow huntsmen – he sometimes conducted his ward rounds in his pink hunting coat before setting off to follow the hounds. He was also a fine shot and a skilful angler. 'Fleming lived two lives,' comments Professor Stanley Graham. 'One life he lived at the children's hospital, and the other among the moors and rivers of Inverness-shire.' The products of his sport on his grouse moor near Tomatin, and on the stretch of the Findhorn where he caught salmon with trout rods, were generously distributed among the staff at Yorkhill.

As yet another of the hospital's philanthropic bachelors, Fleming was generous, too, with his money – contributing to various good causes, especially those connected with the welfare of children. He was also a generous host. 'He would ask a few friends to dine,' recalled a colleague, 'and with good food and good wine recall to mind the more spacious days before the First World War.' His courtesy also belonged to an earlier age, and it was said that 'he was never heard to speak ill of anyone'.

★   ★   ★

The ebullient Noah Morris was the first man to hold the combined post of university lecturer in biochemistry and biochemist at the children's hospital. Morris was still in his early 30s when he took up his Yorkhill appointment in 1928. Nine years later he was to become Professor of Materia Medica at Glasgow University and physician at Stobhill Hospital, and his name was to become associated with the development of geriatrics as well as paediatrics. But it was as Yorkhill's biochemist that he first built up his considerable reputation for research work; and it was here, too, that he first demonstrated his flair for inspiring his assistants – whose researches resulted in many important contributions to medical literature. 'He was most happy at Yorkhill, where most of his real productive work was done,' noted John Blacklock, who was pathologist at the children's hospital when Morris was biochemist. Undaunted by the limitations of the small biochemistry department on the roof of the hospital, he undertook important work on the biochemical problems of disease in the early years of life: notably on the metabolism of phosphorus and calcium and on acid-base balance.

Morris had, recalls one of his colleagues, 'a bursting interest in everything in life.' Jovial and talkative, full of zest and enthusiasm, he always seemed to be 'the centre of a group gathered round to hear his latest sally'. He had a reputation as a witty and stimulating teacher, and a flair for administration: with his blunt speech and forthright opinions he had a strong influence on university affairs. When he died in 1947, only in his early 50s, it was remarked that 'with no particular advantage of birth and upbringing and no outstanding quality of appearance and address he nevertheless attained a position of immense esteem in the academic and medical world'.

★   ★   ★

Paediatric surgery, like medicine, was making great strides at Yorkhill in these years; and constantly in the forefront of advances in this field were the names of Alexander MacLennan, William Rankin, and Matthew White.

Alexander MacLennan, the first Barclay lecturer in surgery, is one of the outstanding figures in Yorkhill's history. The son of a silk merchant, he was educated at Glasgow High School and Glasgow University, where he was the most distinguished graduate of his year. Before the First World War he worked as an assistant at the West Graham Street dispensary; and for almost the whole of the inter-war period he was Barclay lecturer and senior surgeon at

Yorkhill, where his clinics became a centre of pioneer work in surgical paediatrics.

MacLennan was a magnificent surgeon – astute, quick, neat, inventive, bursting with ideas, turning his hand to surgery of all kinds – plastic, orthopaedic, abdominal, ear nose and throat, even tooth-pulling when the occasion demanded; and he was also an expert medical photographer. As an operator he possessed, it was said, 'the sure delicacy of touch essential in children's surgery.' And children loved him. 'He had the most wonderful ability to handle the sick child, and patients in his wards had a magnificent outlook,' comments Miss Olivia Robinson, former matron, who recalls in particular one small girl who, receiving operation after operation from MacLennan, 'just adored him.'

Something of a ritual in the operating theatre was MacLennan's preliminary sharpening of his knife on a stone. The usual practice in these days before disposable blades was to send the knives away for sharpening, but MacLennan preferred to see to it himself that his knife was really sharp. He also favoured French wire nails, at a penny a dozen, rather than the orthodox nickel-plated pins used for elbow fractures. The nails were rusty when they came out but apparently did no harm. There was nothing archaic about the actual operations – MacLennan's technique for pinning the elbow joints was a notable advance.

A few years after his arrival at Yorkhill, MacLennan, recognising the importance in a children's hospital of the manufacture and repair of special splints, set up one of the first splint departments in British hospitals. With his natural flair for mechanics he also maintained excellent workshops both at the hospital and at his home, producing many ingenious devices which he successfully applied to the orthopaedic treatment of children. Many of them were the prototypes of modern appliances.

In orthopaedic surgery generally he had a special interest, and he was an enthusiastic advocate of its development at Yorkhill. At the hospital's annual meeting in 1925 he remarked that the reputation of Glasgow was unfortunate in that walking the streets were perhaps a greater number of cripples than in any other city in the Empire. This was, he added, 'a disgrace to our city and to our civilisation.' The new orthopaedics department then being planned at Yorkhill was, MacLennan thought, a serious attempt to grapple

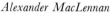
Alexander MacLennan   *Matthew White*

with this problem. It was indeed with a certain amount of fanfare that a jubilee orthopaedic appeal for £50,000 was launched in 1932, and MacLennan set off on a tour of foreign orthopaedic centres to garner the latest ideas. Later, however, doubts grew about the desirability of this kind of sub-specialisation, and it was not until well after the Second World War that orthopaedics developed at Yorkhill on the scale MacLennan had envisaged.

Passionately interested in the technique of surgery, MacLennan also carried his craftsmanship into his private life – carpentry was his hobby.

Alex. MacLennan set high standards for himself and for others, but, though he could be biting on occasion, he is remembered as a courteous and thoroughly kindly man, and one who showed such confidence in his juniors that he put them in charge of wards. 'It was like a death in the hospital when he left,' recalls one of his former assistants.

Matthew White, MacLennan's surgical colleague in the 1930s and his successor in the Barclay lectureship from 1939 to 1953, has been described as 'one of Yorkhill's most lovable characters'. White's first association with the hospital was not as a doctor but as a patient: invalided home from Italy he was one of the occupants of the military wards in 1916. Eight years later he became a junior member of the hospital staff, and in 1930, at the age of 41, he was made surgeon in charge of wards. Described once as 'the doyen of children's surgery in Scotland' White was a paediatric pioneer in the surgery of the thorax and one of the first men to obtain some success in the abdominal surgery of the newborn. He published works on almost every branch of children's surgery and was co-author of the first undergraduate textbook on the subject in English.

White was a man of wide outlook and interests. In his student days he had been a crony of O. H. Mavor and Walter Elliot at Glasgow University – and was also president of the Student Christian Movement. He graduated in arts as well as in medicine, having studied concurrently Greek and zoology; moral philosophy and natural philosophy; and English literature and chemistry. In later life he was sometimes referred to as 'the man who took Greek and zoology at the same time'. He was yet another of Yorkhill's distinguished bachelors.

White had a great enthusiasm for motor cars, beginning at the age of 17 with an 8 h.p. Darracq. The present Barclay lecturer in paediatric surgery, Mr Wallace Dennison, has recorded that 'in 1933, at the age of 44, Matthew White found the current motor cars rather sluggish and took his pilot's certificate. His house surgeons basking in the sunshine on the roof of the children's hospital found it rather disconcerting to see their Chief swooping down on them in his Gypsy Moth'.

★　　★　　★

Coming about Yorkhill in those inter-war years were men who remembered the hospital in the 1880s and others who were to know it in the 1970s. Barclay Ness and Robert Parry, once Garnethill housemen, were now Yorkhill consultants; and among many younger men who were to reach the peak of their careers after the Second World War were two future occupants of the Samson Gemmell Chair – Dr Stanley Graham, who was appointed to wards in 1930, and his professorial successor Dr James Hutchison, who became a house physician in 1934 and afterwards dispensary physician.

Others had a more short-lived connection with the hospital. There were some whose Yorkhill careers were cut unexpectedly short: William Rankin, distinguished and imperturbable surgeon in the

1920s, resigned after a disagreement over the regulations on the appointment and duties of assistants; and Douglas Macfarlane, young surgical protegé of Alexander MacLennan, died of coronary thrombosis not long after being appointed to wards.

Some were later to rise to eminence outside Yorkhill and paediatrics – Professor Dugald Baird of Aberdeen University was Rankin's house surgeon in 1924; Professor Andrew Kay, of the Regius Chair of Surgery at Glasgow University, was a houseman in 1940. A few were to find fame outside the world of medicine altogether. Dr O. H. Mavor, otherwise James Bridie, was a dispensary physician from 1924 to 1927, when he resigned to take up his appointment as Professor of Medicine at the Anderson College. James Greenlees (who along with Harry Hutchieson, also of Glasgow, and Leonard Findlay was among the founders of the Scottish Paediatric Society in 1922) had earlier found fame as a rugby internationalist and later he was to leave medicine to become headmaster of Loretto. (He also became an energetic chairman of the Royal Hospital for Sick Children, Edinburgh.) Ian MacPherson had been the only surviving officer of the Rifle Brigade at Passchendaele, and another senior surgeon, J. P. ('Pim') Fleming, second in command to Matthew White, had served on the *Lion* at Jutland.

The number of women on the Yorkhill medical staff would have pleased the pioneering spirit of Dr Alice McLaren, former dispensary doctor. Among them was Dr Agnes Cameron, who had joined the visiting staff of the children's dispensary before the First World War. Dr Cameron, who now lives in retirement in Ayr, enrolled as a medical student at Queen Margaret College in 1900. She still vividly recalls the long treks from the college to her early-morning pathology class at the Royal Infirmary – there being no tram service between the two points. She has many memories, too, of working with Leonard Findlay at the children's dispensary in the pre-1914 era. Findlay sometimes had occasion to chide mothers for not carrying out his instructions; and Dr Cameron recalls how one such mother emerged from an interview with Findlay, leaned helplessly against the door, and declared: 'I'm glad I'm no' married to *that* man!' Dr Cameron was one of the depleted staff who bore the heavy burden of dispensary work during the First World War. 'I would sometimes see as many as 80 cases between 10 a.m. and 2 p.m.,' she recalls.

Younger doctors included also Dr Mary Stevenson, an arts graduate who later returned to university to study medicine. Her visits to rickets sufferers had helped propel her towards paediatrics and she became a member of the Yorkhill staff from 1923 to the end of the Second World War. Dr Stevenson, who was one of Leonard Findlay's assistants, recalls that he was the first to diagnose encephalitis lethargica, the sleeping sickness that was epidemic in Europe in the mid-1920s. Findlay, however, chose to submit his findings to a minor publication, with the result that the credit later went to doctors on the Continent. Glasgow had its share of sufferers from this disease. 'Some of the most distressing cases are those suffering from the after-effects of sleeping sickness, which affects the mental condition,' noted the Yorkhill almoner in 1926.

To the considerable Yorkhill corpus of specialised knowledge on everything from Greek to grouse-shooting, Dr Elaine Stocquart, senior anaesthetist for many years, certainly contributed her quota. Dr Stocquart, who joined the staff of Yorkhill in 1929 and was consultant anaesthetist at the hospital before her retiral in 1960, was brought up in Belgium and came to Glasgow in the First World War, where she has lived ever since. She had studied at the Brussels Conservatory, and one surgeon recalls how Dr Stocquart and a colleague sometimes arrived at the operating theatre discussing medieval French history – in French. As a skilled horsewoman she used to take almost the entire surgical unit out riding on the hills beyond Mugdock; only Matthew White, presumably considering horses a little lumbering in comparison with Gypsy Moths, absented himself from these weekly surgical cavalcades of the late 1930s.

Over this rich array of talent and personality there presided the medical superintendent, David Campbell Suttie. Suttie had gone to New Zealand early in his career, and on his return to Scotland was appointed to the new medical superintendent's post which had been created when Yorkhill opened in 1914. Apart from service in the First World War he remained at the hospital till his retirement in 1953, combining the posts of superintendent and radiologist.

The medical superintendent, in those days before regional boards, exercised a very close control over the hospital's visiting staff; and Campbell Suttie's reign at Yorkhill was not only long but fairly stringent. Sharp-eyed, and of impressive girth, he had also on occasion a crushing turn of phrase. 'Doctor,' he would say, 'a rose

has fallen from your chaplet – you've left the bunsen burner on.'
Despite his essential kindness he was a strict disciplinarian. His post
as radiologist, moreover, gave him a chance to assess the work of the
surgeons – he could see the results on his X-ray plates. Residents
were also kept firmly under his thumb. Once, when a houseman took
the liberty of phoning the superintendent's house at midnight to
wish him a merry Christmas, Suttie came hotfoot to the hospital in
a vain attempt to discover the culprit.

Suttie, who married late in life, lived in a house acquired by the
hospital in University Avenue – it had formerly been the house of
J. J. Burnet, architect of Yorkhill, and was later to become a psychia-
tric day unit for Yorkhill. During the Second World War, however,
he stayed in the hospital in case of emergency, and when a Tannoy
system was installed from his room – echoing the old speaking tubes
of Mrs Harbin's day – Suttie was often to be heard in full cry
through it, sometimes issuing unnecessary summonses simply to test
the system.

He was an efficient administrator, and as a radiologist he was
noted particularly for his diagnosis of bone diseases. After his
retirement from Yorkhill he continued to work as a locum radiologist
for the brief period before his death.

Chapter 16

VIEW FROM THE BOARDROOM

SWEEPING administrative as well as medical changes followed the opening of the new hospital on Yorkhill. The old constitution was considered too narrow for the hospital in its new and more important role and in 1922 a new one, shelved during the war years, came into force. The hospital was incorporated as a company, taking as its corporate seal a miniature of Raphael's Sistine Madonna; and the directorate was broadened to include representatives of public bodies and leading institutions. There were to be two directors representing the factories and warehouses which subscribed to the hospital; two representing the university; two from Glasgow Corporation. Other local authorities were also represented, as well as the Royal Faculty of Physicians and Surgeons of Glasgow, the Merchants' House, the Trades House, and the Glasgow Education Department. In addition 15 directors, at least four of them women, were elected by the hospital governors. All regular subscribers of a guinea or more could apply to become governors.

The works representatives were chosen at a meeting of employees, and if voting became necessary each delegate had a vote for every £1 subscribed by his works in the previous year. At these meetings an account was given of the hospital's work, questions were answered, and a brief lecture given. In 1927, for example, delegates listened to a short address by Barclay Ness on rheumatism in childhood.

Two chairmen spanned the inter-war years – Charles K. Aitken up to 1931 and Robert F. Barclay after him. Between them they held this office for nearly 40 years, and Aitken's chairmanship, from 1909 till 1931, is the longest in the hospital's history.

Aitken, a native of Glasgow, became a member of the Glasgow Stock Exchange Association in 1875 and was several times its chairman. He played a prominent part in promoting various reforms in its business methods, and at the age of 80 was made a life member of the exchange. When not dealing in stocks and shares or engaged in hospital business he was often to be found in the vicinity of a golf course. He was a member of the Royal and Ancient for more than 50 years and captain of Prestwick Golf Club at the turn of the century.

Robert Barclay in 1935

Aitken took over the chairmanship of the board at a crucial period in the hospital's history, when architects and contractors were being appointed for the new building at Yorkhill; and during his chairmanship £300,000 was raised and expended on land, building, and equipment. He was a courteous, dignified man and made a diplomatic chairman; during his period of office board meetings were, the annual report commented on his retiral, 'like a family party, and any ill feeling over a difference of opinion was unknown.'

In any discussion of the hospital's history three names are likely to recur – James Nicoll, Leonard Findlay, and Robert Barclay. Barclay, who succeeded Aitken as chairman in 1931, first joined the board in the closing years of the nineteenth century. It was natural enough that as a young solicitor in Andrew Macgeorge's old firm he should become interested in an institution served by so many of his colleagues. But there was also a more personal and compelling force behind his work for the hospital. Poliomyelitis in childhood, when he was pulled through by the family doctor, had left him permanently lame; it had also left him with a lasting interest in the welfare of sick children.

At the turn of the century Barclay became honorary secretary of the hospital, and played the leading role in its transformation from a converted dwelling house on Garnethill to a new and modern hospital on the Yorkhill site. It was during his years as secretary, too, that in 1919 he endowed the Barclay lectureship in the surgery and orthopaedics of childhood. As chairman from 1931 to 1946 – he resigned two years before his death – he became a recognised authority on voluntary hospitals; and as chairman of the Scottish branch of the British Hospitals Association he led the campaign to preserve the independence of the voluntary hospitals within the proposed nationalised framework.

Educated at Glasgow High School and Glasgow University – which conferred upon him the honorary degree of LL.D. in 1935 – Barclay was a big, burly man, comparable in girth with Campbell Suttie: the two of them made an imposing pair as they rode together in Suttie's tiny Austin 7. Barclay himself never drove a car; but in his younger days he used to arrive at work in style – riding down on horseback from his Park Terrace home to his office in the city centre. His groom would lead the horse away – and reappear in time for the homeward journey.

Robert Barclay had a patient's eye view of the children's hospital in 1921, when he broke his leg outside the building. When Campbell Suttie, who was with him, inquired which hospital the honorary secretary wished to be taken to, Barclay replied: 'I'm at the hospital. Take me inside.' There he remained for some weeks, in a room next to the boardroom and under the care of William Rankin. And when some time later he again broke his leg he had no hesitation in saying to Suttie: 'If you did me once, you can do me again.'

Like Barclay, Alan Clapperton, honorary treasurer of the hospital for 36 years, was a partner in the firm of solicitors which through the years and under a variety of names had remained so closely associated with the hospital.

Clapperton, educated at Uppingham under the celebrated Dr
Thring, was secretary of Glasgow University Court for more than
40 years and edited the two volumes of the Ordinances of the
Scottish Universities. Renowned for his close knowledge of the
development of academic institutions, he 'could always tell, without
notice, the respects in which the Scottish universities varied in law
or in custom'; and there wasn't much in the history of Glasgow
University that he didn't know. It was said that 'few men were
better known in academic, legal, and hospital circles'. Music was
another of his interests, and he became a director of the Scottish
National Academy of Music.

Alan Clapperton

After Clapperton's resignation close links with Glasgow University
were still maintained at board level, as the new constitution ensured;
and for a quarter of a century the impressive tones of Professor
Edward P. Cathcart, of the Chair of Physiology, were frequently to
be heard in the deliberations of the board and its committees.
Cathcart, who was one of the university's representatives on the
board from 1922 to 1947, was recently described by Sir Charles
Illingworth as 'volcanic, generous, warm-hearted, applying his deep
voice in equal measure to giving hospitable welcome, pouring scorn
upon a new theory, or denouncing an injustice'.

126

The board had, indeed, links with most spheres of Glasgow life, including the press. Between 1924 and 1935 Sir Robert Bruce, editor of *The Glasgow Herald*, was an extremely active director. Bruce had taken up his appointment as editor within a few weeks of the opening of the new hospital – which he once went so far as to describe as 'a children's fairy palace on a hill.'

★   ★   ★

When Clapperton died in 1935 it was noted that during the 36 years of his treasurership the annual revenue of the hospital had increased from £5000 to £50,000. With the finances and administration growing more complex it was decided in 1931 – when Robert Barclay became chairman as well as honorary secretary – that a full-time secretary should be appointed. Mr James Methven, a young law agent with Robert Barclay's firm, was appointed to the post, moving into a new and larger office acquired by the hospital in St Vincent Street. This was a significant appointment: Mr Methven, a native of Fife, was to remain at the hospital – with only a break for war service – until his retiral in 1968, and on the introduction of the National Health Service became secretary to the hospital group to which Yorkhill belonged. At the same time it was decided to have a comprehensive organisation for collections, and Mr J. Glen Boyd was appointed full-time organising collector with responsibility for all subscriptions and donations made throughout Scotland (and occasionally beyond) with the exception of the ladies' committee's collections. He, too, was to remain with the hospital till after the introduction of the National Health Service.

The hospital's system of subscriptions was now well established, and even during the Depression years there was, Mr Methven recalls, no marked falling away of contributions.

A hospital report in the 1930s suggested that 'some wealthy men and women are beginning to realise that it is much better to experience the joy of giving rather than the pain of being taxed'. However, although the hospital to some extent built up its funds through private approaches to individuals, money came from far and wide and from rich and poor. The proceeds of backcourt concerts found their way into the Yorkhill coffers; so did the contents of 'Pollok contract swear-box' (7s 6d in 1938), and the entrance money to the annual billiard tournament in the smokeroom of Miss Cranston's tearoom. In the early days of Garnethill money had been raised at Victorian sermons and musical soirees; now, in the '20s and '30s, it came from whist drives and bridge contests and bowling tournaments; and among the gifts in kind, rocking horses were supplanted by Hornby trains. A model of the new *Queen Mary* (launched at Clydebank in 1934), cigarette cards, comics, and toy motor cars were among other gifts. Flowers and fruit still arrived in abundance, however; the Tharsis company continued to send their crates of oranges, and an annual gift of grapes came from the Queen. In 1929 a gift of pottery from the Duchess of York included 120 porridge bowls bearing pictures of Princess Elizabeth.

There were gifts of medical equipment, too; and in the late '30s, Yorkhill took advantage of Lord Nuffield's offer to provide every hospital in the country with an iron lung.

Important sources of income continued to include legacies, endowments, and interest on investments. In 1932, the hospital's jubilee year, there were 45 legacies for general purposes, ranging from £1 to £30,300; seven cots were endowed and five named; the revenue from investments was £14,000; and subscriptions amounted to £16,000. The hospital's income that year was £31,000 and the expenditure £43,000, the balance being made up as usual from the extraordinary funds.

The ladies' committee, under the leadership of women like Mrs R. Cleland Gourlay, honorary secretary, soldiered on in their collection of subscriptions – they raised £1100 in 1932. Until the early 1930s the committee, now 30-strong, included one of the members of the original ladies' association formed in 1883 – Miss Anna Reid, who was president from 1920 to 1931, two years before her death.

Children, too, continued to play their part – the Children's Tinfoil League was formed to collect silver paper and lead for sale in bulk for the benefit of the hospital. There were several other new sources of regular income. When Queen Alexandra became a patroness of the hospital she granted authority for an annual collection, and Queen Alexandra Rose Day was started in 1914, with small pink roses on sale in all districts of the city. The 1920s saw the beginning of the annual Glasgow students' charities days, and the hospital received a handsome share of the takings. In 1926 the directors thanked the students for their 'remembrance of the sick kids' in endowing the Glasgow Students' Charities Day cot. The Central Station 'Shell', a polished relic of the First World War which was the gift of Lord Invernairn, a patron of the hospital – was another regular source of revenue, and in 1935 it was noted that contributions there on behalf of Yorkhill 'considerably exceeded' those in the 'shells' at St Enoch and Queen Street stations on behalf of other hospitals.

Parents of patients were also encouraged to contribute when possible. In 1919 the hospital almoner was instructed to 'tactfully sound them as to their ability and willingness' to make donations. There was much talk in these years of opening a separate department for paying patients – Alexander MacLennan was a strong advocate of this – but no definite steps had been taken in this direction before the outbreak of war in 1939.

Increasingly, in the inter-war years, funds were started for special purposes – the extension fund of 1924, the jubilee orthopaedic fund, the research fund of 1929. When this last appeal – for £20,000 – was launched it was pointed out that the money for lectureships associated with the hospital went to the university – but the hospital provided the facilities.

Chapter 17

SOMETHING TO CELEBRATE

THE jubilee of 1932 was an occasion for celebration – 100 people dined on roast pheasant at a dinner given by Robert Barclay at the Royal Scottish Automobile Club. It was also a time for statistics. No fewer than 112,000 children had passed through the wards since 1883, and some striking comparisons could be made between Garnethill in the 1880s and Yorkhill 50 years on. At Garnethill in the first year of the hospital's history 263 patients had been treated; now, at Yorkhill, almost as many were treated each day. In the mid-1880s it had cost about £5 a day to run the hospital; now it cost about £4 an hour. In 1883 there was a medical and surgical staff of 12; now there were more than 70. A handful of students had put in an appearance at Garnethill in the early years; now all medical students were obliged to attend as part of their course – and from the mid-30s written and clinical exams were held twice yearly at Yorkhill as part of the finals. One thing had not changed, however: there was still never a vacant bed.

Even since the opening of Yorkhill in 1914 there had been great changes. Medical electricity, for example, was still in its infancy in 1914; by the mid-'30s the hospital had apparatus for ultra-violet rays and infra-red rays, and the old X-ray machine, once considered the best to be had, was now obsolete. The pathology department had expanded from tiny beginnings under John W. S. Blacklock, first Gardiner lecturer and Yorkhill pathologist for 13 years till he left in 1937 to take up his post as St Mungo-Notman Professor of Pathology at Glasgow University; and under Noah Morris biochemistry had made great advances. Another sign of the times was the appointment in 1931 of honorary consultants in psychology and neurological surgery.

Clinics for the treatment of former patients had become an established part of the hospital's work – the rheumatism clinic, the diabetics clinic, the chest clinic, the renal clinic. On the suggestion of Matthew White a speech clinic was started at the dispensary in 1936 under Dr Anne McAllister, of Jordanhill Training College, for the benefit of children who had been operated on for cleft palate and hare lip. Another inter-war innovation at the dispensary was the department for treating skin diseases.

The hospital's splint department, meanwhile, was continuing to grow in importance. Tentatively begun in 1919, it had been built up by Miss Sophia Muirhead into 'a really skilled, scientific, and essential part of the hospital'. By the 1930s splints were being made from fibre instead of celluloid, and it was possible to manufacture special unbreakable splints which could be scrubbed with soap and water. Appliances produced at Yorkhill ranged from surgical corsets and boots to tin head splints. Miss Muirhead – 'a genius at working out ideas with extreme accuracy,' in the words of one doctor – had spent several months in London studying the most up-to-date methods of splint manufacture.

The long war continued to be waged against tuberculosis, broncho-pneumonia, infantile gastroenteritis, and the problems of incorrect artificial feeding. In 1933 there were 204 cases of gastroenteritis in the wards, 82 of them fatal; 126 cases of pneumonia; and 69 of broncho-pneumonia (including 49 fatal cases, almost all in babies under one year old). Other familiar enemies included nephritis, the common kidney disease; and marasmus, the progressive wasting disease from which, even in 1933, less than half the victims recovered. Osteomyelitis was the scourge of the surgical wards and one-third of the victims died.

But now the battle was being fought in the laboratories as well as in the wards. Research continued to forge ahead at Yorkhill in the 1930s under the two medical chiefs, Geoffrey Fleming and Dr (later Professor) Stanley Graham, who were supported in the biochemistry laboratory by Noah Morris and in pathology by John Blacklock. 'The common ailments of that time are reflected in the research interests upon which these men built their not inconsiderable reputations,' notes Professor James Hutchison. 'Fleming's work on

131

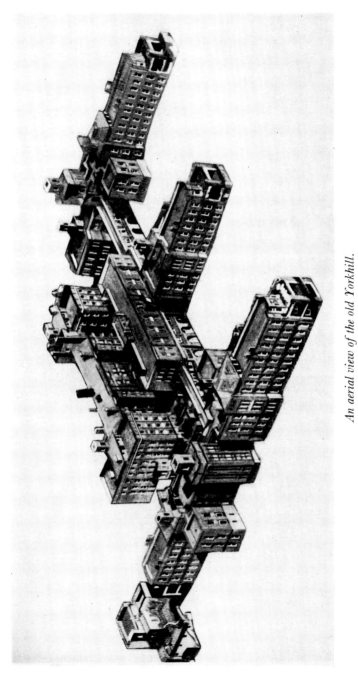

An aerial view of the old Yorkhill.

the scientific basis of infant feeding must have saved many lives at a time when death was frequently attributable to incorrect artificial feeding. The basic studies by Graham and Morris into *Acidosis and Alkalosis* (the title of their classic textbook) helped to reduce the appalling mortality which resulted from such diseases as infantile gastroenteritis, pyloric stenosis, and acute renal failure. Blacklock's work on childhood tuberculosis can be related to the high incidence and mortality from this disease in the '30s, and for long afterwards.'

Despite these advances, and despite extremely high clinical and nursing standards, there was still little effective treatment for the many severe infections that filled the wards – pneumonia, cerebrospinal meningitis, tuberculosis, pyelonephritis, osteomyelitis, and gastroenteritis. The conquest of most of those diseases awaited the development of modern drugs after the Second World War, though in 1936 there was an important breakthrough when the first sulphonamide was introduced into therapeutics and, in the words of Professor Hutchison, 'almost overnight cerebrospinal meningitis lost its terrors.' Neonatal medicine, too, had still far to go; in the 1930s paediatricians still played only a minor role in the care of the newborn in maternity hospitals, and the causes of many neonatal deaths remained obscure.

★   ★   ★

Paediatric surgery, under MacLennan and White, also continued to advance in the 1930s. Operations increased in number and variety, and there were more accident cases than ever before. Each year hundreds of children were treated for burns and scalds, and the first burns unit in Scotland was established at the hospital, with Mr Wallace Dennison in charge. In 1937 it was noted that the greater number of motor cars on the roads was among the causes of growing demands on the time of the surgical staff; whereas a quarter of a century before a visiting surgeon might have spent a couple of hours at the hospital every morning now he was in attendance all morning and often in the afternoon and evening, and during the night 'in connection with accident and emergency cases'. More than 5000 operations were performed in the hospital that year. More than 100 children were treated for poliomyelytis, more than 300 for burns and scalds, more than 400 for fractures; about 400 appendices were removed – and one pair of Siamese twins were separated. There was only one tracheostomy, the commonest emergency operation in the early years on Garnethill; and only three blood transfusions were given, a commonplace emergency measure at Yorkhill today. One old enemy which had now lost most of its sting was pyloric stenosis, an obstruction of the stomach outlet caused by over-development of muscle fibre and affecting babies – especially males – in the first few weeks of life. At the children's dispensary before the First World War James Nicoll had pioneered a plastic operation for this disease; and now a Continental refinement on Nicoll's technique, Ramstedt's operation, was achieving a high success rate – 75 children underwent this operation at Yorkhill in 1937, with 62 complete recoveries. Rammstedt's technique had been hit on largely by accident, after one operation along Nicoll's lines had to be abandoned when incomplete – with unexpectedly successful results.

It was in 1937, too, that hopes were first raised of the establishment of a university Chair in paediatric surgery to match the Gemmell Chair in medical paediatrics. Fred H. Young, of James Templeton and Co., the Glasgow carpet manufacturers, offered £80,000 to found a university chair of orthopaedic surgery in association with the hospital; an ordinance was actually drafted – but the proposal ran into opposition and was abandoned. Later in the year however, the offer was made in a different form, and the visiting surgeons of the three infirmaries and of the children's hospital met under the chairmanship of Professor Archibald Young, of the Chair of Surgery, to discuss its terms. They unanimously agreed that the proposed chair would benefit neither the children's hospital nor the study of orthopaedic surgery, since this was essentially a post-graduate subject. A better idea, they thought, would be to replace the Barclay lectureship with a Chair of surgical paediatrics and a lectureship in orthopaedics associated with the hospital. This was as far as the matter got: first Alex. MacLennan and then Professor Young retired, and war broke out. The proposals never reached the Senate.

*   *   *

Mrs Louisa Harbin, the hospital's first matron, was still alive and following the fortunes of the hospital with interest in the jubilee year. Yorkhill in 1932 must have seemed to her a far cry from Garnethill

The nurses' sitting-room.

Scene in one of the wards between the wars.

135

half a century before, with its speaking tubes, its gas-lit operating theatre, and its cramped nurses' quarters. After the extensions of the 1920s the accommodation for nurses included a lecture hall, a recreation room large enough for dancing or for badminton, and a large sitting room – one of the splendours of the old Yorkhill – with a stage at one end for the annual shows. The nurses' bedrooms occupied the top floors of the two new wings and, as one journal reported, 'those who appreciate the fresh air can take their beds out on to the flat roof that covers the new quarters.'

The old stiff collars and cuffs gave way in 1930 to a new uniform with soft Peter Pan collars – the change being made after two nurses had modelled the old and the new uniforms at a board meeting.

More was changing than appearances. With the establishment of the General Nursing Council in 1919, a special register for children's nurses was started – Robert Barclay being closely concerned in the campaign for this. A three-year training curriculum, conforming with the lines laid down by the G.N.C., was introduced at Yorkhill, and in 1922 a Sister tutor was appointed.

With increasing numbers of infants being treated at the hospital, and with the reduction of working hours, many more nurses were needed and by the early '20s there were 100 probationers on the staff. There was no shortage of recruits in those years: 777 applied in 1932. Because of the nature of the work nurses at Yorkhill were able to start their training at a rather earlier age than was the case in the general hospitals. In the late 1930s the disturbingly high proportion of nurses on the sick list was put down partly to 'the fact that the visiting surgeons made a practice of sending these young nurses to bed as a precautionary measure even though there was not much the matter with them'.

Many nurses of the inter-war period are still vividly remembered today. Presiding over the dispensary from 1923 to 1948 was Sister Laura's successor, Sister Jane Turnbull – a knowledgeable, well-read, highly capable woman who was, in the words of a former matron, 'quite a power in the land.' Sometimes, in the absence of the surgeons, Sister Turnbull undertook minor operations, administering the anaesthetic herself. As Sister in charge of the dispensary she was also responsible for ordering the food – and once, called to account for ordering fresh salmon, she replied: 'Well, there's no waste in salmon.' Well remembered also are Sister Bamber, the Englishwoman who as first Sister tutor established the nursing school at Yorkhill (she died only a few years ago, at the age of 96) and Sister Isabel Neilson, the X-ray Sister. Sister Isabel spent her whole working life at Yorkhill, retiring in 1947. A more fleeting appearance was put in by the matron-elect of a new hospital to be opened in Johannesburg, who was sent to Glasgow for special training. And there was even a time when Yorkhill's nursing staff included a Sister called Florence Nightingale.

Miss Olivia Robinson

There were two matrons in the inter-war period – Miss Mary Cameron and her successor, Miss M. Olivia Robinson. Mary Cameron, who trained at the Western Infirmary, was matron at Sunderland Children's Infirmary before coming to Yorkhill in 1917 to take up the post so suddenly vacated by Julia Simpson. A large, majestic, good-looking woman with a Highland accent, Miss Cameron was one of the old school of matrons. Born in Corpach, she belonged to a nursing family – her three sisters were all nurses too. Like Campbell Suttie, the medical superintendent, she was both efficient and something of a disciplinarian. This was an age when nurses' holidays could still be, and sometimes were, cancelled with the words: 'Nonsense, nurse – go back to your ward. We're short of nurses.'

One of the hospital physicians remembers encountering Miss

Cameron as she set off, stick in hand, to join some other matrons for a Sunday afternoon walk. It must, the doctor remembers thinking, have been quite a majestic procession.

In 1933 Miss Cameron became seriously ill, underwent an operation by Alex. MacLennan, and resigned in 1935, dying soon afterwards at the age of 52. Her premature loss was a blow to Yorkhill. 'The personal acquaintance that she had with each child in the hospital was remarkable and invaluable,' acknowledged the directors.

To Yorkhill now as Miss Cameron's successor came Miss Olivia Robinson, from the Hospital for Women in Leeds. She is a native of County Fermanagh, and after training at the Royal Infirmary in Glasgow worked for a time at the Ulster Hospital in Belfast. Miss Robinson is remembered as a popular and highly capable matron, though she remained at the hospital for only six years – in 1941 she left for Edinburgh to take up an appointment at the Department of Health for Scotland, where she later became chief nursing officer. Her reign at Yorkhill, though short, was eventful; in 1941 she played a leading part in the sudden emergency evacuation of the hospital after an air raid had endangered the area.

At Yorkhill Miss Robinson instituted a course of training for probationer nurses on the theory and practice of nursing, which proved useful in enabling them to pass the final State exams. Her own Yorkhill memories are rather of colleagues and patients, and she recalls her first Christmas at the hospital, when she was dismayed to see the children being given their usual diet of mince and milk pudding. On the following years she saw to it that they had a proper Christmas dinner – 'and it was the worst thing I ever did, for it was greeted with a roar of disapproval – "where's the mince?" ' It was in Miss Robinson's day, too, that the first nurses' dance was held at Yorkhill, and she recalls approaching Robert Barclay with this request and being delighted when he not only agreed but added: 'And, Matron, we'll have Joe Loss and his band.'

★   ★   ★

Social work, hitherto in the hands of the dispensary sisters and the ladies' committee, was put on a professional footing with the appointment of a hospital almoner in 1915; and steadily the work grew in importance, chiefly under the influence of Margaret Watson, almoner from 1920 till 1947. Quiet and capable, Miss Watson was a pioneer in the social work of hospital service – and it was, in the words of the directors, 'largely due to her influence that the work became an integral part of the hospital service.' Margaret Watson and her assistants, Charlotte Bannerman and Miss Jane Urie (who later, as head almoner, continued Margaret Watson's pioneering social work), had wide-ranging responsibilities; they interviewed parents at the hospital, organised the special clinics, visited former patients in their homes, and arranged for them to stay at convalescent homes, or to attend special schools, or to visit the country. The problems they faced included, as Margaret Watson put it, 'anything from the payment of a tram fare to problems of real difficulty in family life.' Once help was given to a family living in a condemned house where no repairs were being done – and where the patient was 'a nervous child whose illness was attributed to a fall of plaster from the roof on to her bed'. Prams were lent for the benefit of children hitherto condemned to spend their days in a dark and stuffy kitchen because their mother could not carry them out along with a younger baby. A cot was provided for an infant in a double arm splint, since 'he was a cross and difficult patient and it was impossible for him to continue sharing a bed with the two other children'. A blind boy was given a Braille book to read in bed; children who were unable to walk were taken to the hospital in taxis; and 'a boy who was suffering from the ministrations of an over-anxious mother improved enormously during a month away from home which he spent in the country'.

There was also, sadly, 'the type of child for whom the hospital could do nothing, and who, on discharge, could only be helped by being made as happy and comfortable as possible at home.' Equally, there were social problems outside the power of a hospital almoner to solve. 'The overcrowding problem is beyond us,' wrote Margaret Watson in 1927, 'but we have been able to improve matters in one or two cases by helping to get minor repairs to the house seen to and by the provision of books and clothing.' A frequent problem was that of children who had been treated for chorea – or St Vitus' Dance – and were threatened with a recurrence when they returned to noisy, overcrowded homes. One seven-year-old boy suffering from repeated attacks of this disease was one of a family of nine living in a two-

The conservatory.

The conservatory, with the marble statue of a baby in the foreground.

roomed house in a South-side backland. The house was so dark that the gas lights burned all day, the walls and ceilings were damp, and the kitchen chimney smoky. The father was unable to work because of chronic asthma, and one of the girls was a suspected case of tuberculosis. Since there was no prospect of improved health in these conditions, a successful effort was made in 1929 to find the family a four-roomed house with a tiny garden in one of the new housing estates. In her report Margaret Watson commented: 'Though the rent is heavy the resulting benefit to the whole family has amply justified the experiment. Their somewhat scanty furniture was supplemented by gifts from interested friends and the saving on the gas bill has been a great help towards the larger rent. Our patient is now an ardent gardener and is making steady progress towards recovery.'

The almoner's reports provide a revealing commentary on the social history of the city. The report for 1921, for example, stated: 'The year has been a time of exceptional hardship, and this has naturally been keenly felt in the homes of our hospital patients. A grim succession of strikes, unemployment, and prices that are slow to fall, added to a shortage of suitable houses, have aggravated the conditions of city life which are never too favourable to children. The pinch has perhaps been felt most in the households of thrifty people where the patients have found themselves for the first time unable to pay the rent or provide some necessary but expensive item for a sick child.'

In the Depression years, too, unemployment increased the number of families with no margin of income with which to meet the extra expense of illness; and 1932 was, as Margaret Watson bravely expressed it, 'a time of exceptional opportunity for helping people.' Bad housing had long been a grave problem, but in that year of 1932 a new difficulty had arisen – the family living in a good house whose high rent absorbed more than its fair share of the reduced income. At the chest clinic in those years many patients were found to be suffering from undernourishment and the effects of overcrowding. Children whose mothers had become the family wage earners were often sent to convalescent homes, and Margaret Watson worked in cooperation with the new Unemployment Assistance Board to relieve distress in the homes of patients. In these years many patients came from the counties around Glasgow scheduled as special areas, often from households suffering from the effects of prolonged unemployment.

'It is unfortunately impossible to express adequately in this report what lies behind the cold figures of the year's statistics,' wrote Margaret Watson in 1935. 'Perhaps, however, if they are read in the light of imagination they may show not merely a dry record of work done, but suggest the personal difficulty or the exceptional circumstances which led up to the action taken.' The 'light of imagination' may perhaps be partly supplied by one of Lewis Grassic Gibbon's

The hospital in the early 1930s.

essays of the period, in which he wrote of 150,000 Glaswegians living five or six to a room 'in some great sloven of a tenement – the tenement itself in a line or grouping with hundreds of its fellows, its windows grained with the unceasing wash and drift of coal-dust, its stairs narrow and befouled and steep, its evening breath like that which might issue from the mouth of a diseased beast'.

The almoner and her staff dealt with all manner of problems, grave and less grave, and their responsibility was not confined to the Glasgow area. Once, for example, lodgings were found for 'a distraught mother from Argyll' so that she could stay in the city till her child had recovered from an operation. A temporary home near the hospital was found for a baby from the Western Isles whose

142

parents could not afford to bring him periodically to Yorkhill for the continuous surgical treatment he needed.

The Western Isles, incidentally, were not the limits of the hospital's sphere of activity, and the saga of the patient who travelled to Yorkhill from Iceland makes a romantic passage in the hospital's history. The boy, a blond six-year-old suffering from a cleft palate and hare lip, was the son of a Reykjavik trawler captain who occasionally put in to Leith. The captain had heard of the work being done at Yorkhill, and in due course sailed the boy home again, completely cured. The staff who treated this unusual patient did not know that in a few years the patients at Yorkhill would include children from Poland, Gibraltar, Marseilles, and the Channel Islands – refugees who arrived in Glasgow in the Second World War.

Chapter 18

CHILDREN IN WARTIME

LOOKING across on one side to the neo-Gothic of Gilmorehill, Yorkhill looks down on the other to the cranes and funnels of the river Clyde. The Clyde, like the university, has meant more than a piece of landscape: much of Yorkhill's history has been linked with the fortunes of Clydeside. This was so in the Depression years, as the grim reports of the Yorkhill almoner illustrate, and it was so also in the Second World War. 'The hospital at Yorkhill is regarded as being in the danger zone in respect of its proximity to the Clyde and its prominent position,' ran an ominous official statement quoted in the minutes of 1939.

In the early hours of September 18, 1940, the morning when a stick of bombs landed in George Square, the cruiser *Sussex* at Yorkhill docks, filled with ammunition and ready to sail, was hit by a bomb and set on fire. Doctors watching from the hospital thought at first they were seeing anti-aircraft fire from the cruiser. Standing on one of the ward balconies they saw the cruiser engulfed in thick smoke and then, in the words of Mr A. P. Laird, former Yorkhill surgeon, 'as we watched through the smoke a lazy lick of flame came through and we realised the cruiser had been hit.' Shortly afterwards, recalls the matron, Miss Olivia Robinson, two policemen arrived on the doorstep and said: 'You've got to get the bairns out of this place – it's liable to blow up at any moment.' Though the Govan ferryboat went gallantly into action to fight the flames, the Yorkhill area was endangered by the risk of the ammunition magazine exploding.

The medical superintendent, Campbell Suttie, refused to act on the instructions of the police; but later a call to evacuate the hospital came by telephone from a Department of Health representative; and when Suttie again demurred he was told that this was an order. Evacuation was begun at 6.30 a.m. and was completed by 7.50 a.m., 27 patients being taken by ambulance to the country branch at Drumchapel and the remainder to Mearnskirk Hospital, along with the residents and Sisters in charge of the wards. Four patients, too ill to be moved, remained at the hospital; and four sailors were taken to the out-patient department to be treated for burns. A doctor recalls his amazement on arriving at the hospital that morning to find it empty of children.

The Department of Health congratulated the hospital authorities on 'the very satisfactory and expeditious way in which the evacuation had been carried through,' and the medical superintendent and matron were praised for the arrangements they had made for such an eventuality. The matron, Miss Robinson, adds a strange footnote to the episode. At dinner on the very night of the raid something, she recalls, made her ask the housekeeping Sister to 'have a quiet talk to the nurses and tell them they should pack a few belongings in case of evacuation'. The nurses' interpretation of 'a few belongings' was such that the corridors were soon jammed with trunks, and a more modest re-packing had to be requested.

Within a year it was the turn of the country branch. Early in May 1941, several landmines exploded outside the building, extensively damaging the plaster-work and doors and leaving scarcely a pane of glass intact. Despite 'the terrific nature of the explosion' not one of the 50 children and 30 members of staff was injured. The fortunate escape of the children was attributed to 'the fact that, as arranged, each child had been enclosed in a sort of tent made by a heavy coverlet laid over the sides of the cot' (a system also used at the hospital, and highly popular with the patients). The Drumchapel children were temporarily evacuated to Lennox Hospital. Sister Edith Charles – who was Sister in charge of the country branch for 16 years before her retiral in 1945 – and the rest of the staff were praised for 'their courage and resource in very trying and dangerous circumstances'. And at the next annual meeting of the hospital Lord Provost 'Paddy' Dollan remarked that if the Clydeside riveter had been compared with a Grenadier Guardsman under fire, it was equally true that the Clydeside nurse had been in the firing line and had shown undaunted courage.

Yorkhill stayed civilian in this war; no wards were taken over by the military authorities, no Captain Gracie appeared on the scene. But day-to-day life in the hospital, quite apart from air raids and the temporary evacuation, was far from normal. Blackout and poor lighting hampered work in the wards; there was a serious coal shortage; the water pressure was so low that supplies failed to reach the top floor and a booster pump had to be installed. A strip of the hospital ground had to be given up for a shelter trench for soldiers at Yorkhill drill hall, despite Robert Barclay's protests that this was against the spirit of the Geneva Convention. And the hospital, meanwhile, looked to its own defences, with shelters near the tennis courts, a gas de-contamination chamber, and a protective wall. Nurses attended lectures on fire-fighting and anti-gas treatment; and the normal nursing staff was supplemented by auxiliary nurses, including members of the Ranger movement. With voluntary drivers of private cars hard to come by, children were sometimes brought to hospital by British and American Red Cross transport units. The Christmas treat was cancelled. Geoffrey Fleming gave up his car as a contribution to the war effort – and was later disconcerted to see one of his colleagues driving around in it. And a new plea was heard in the wards, on the morning after a raid – 'Have ye nae shrapnel?'

Refugees arrived from Europe, and evacuees from the bombed areas at home. A child who had contracted infantile paralysis on a refugee boat from Gibraltar was provided with a splint; a small Londoner suffering from bomb hysteria was sent to a convalescent home. On the brighter side, there were reports of seriously debilitated children who used to attend Yorkhill clinics and were now, as evacuees in the country, thriving and putting on weight.

Throughout the war a number of cots were reserved for possible air raid casualties. In the event, these were not used – though patients included such wartime casualties as the two boys who had found a hand grenade in the Kilpatrick Hills. In the first months of the war, with 80 cots out of commission, the nurses had more time than usual on their hands – extra table tennis sets and card tables were purchased, theatricals and country dances arranged. This was a short-lived problem. As the war dragged on, nurses were increasingly thin on the ground, and after a national appeal to Sisters to serve abroad there were difficulties in training recruits. As in the First World War, many doctors were absent on military service or in the emergency hospitals, their absence placing a strain on those who remained. Domestic staff were in increasingly short supply, and by the end of the war the domestic wing was completely unoccupied.

Altogether it was a difficult time for the hospital. 'There are many children who are not receiving the treatment their condition demands and that they would receive in normal times,' stated the annual report for 1944 – a year when a serious outbreak of gastroenteritis raised the already high infantile death rate in the city. This was a time when the findings of John Boyd Orr's committee on infantile mortality had heightened public concern on the subject. Of 17 countries Scotland had the highest rate, 77 per 1000, and Glasgow's was the highest rate of any British city – 57 per cent higher than Birmingham, 27 per cent higher than Liverpool. As in the days when the hospital's Victorian founders were launching their campaign, the causes of mortality were social and economic as well as medical. Now the directors echoed a distressingly familiar Glasgow refrain when they commented: 'The panacea for high infant mortality can be stated in two words – good homes, in the fullest sense of that term.'

Chapter 19

NATIONAL HEALTH

NOT one but two sets of directors gathered in the boardroom on July 5, 1948; and when the meeting dispersed Yorkhill's days as a voluntary hospital were over. Under the National Health Act control of the hospital passed to the Western Regional Hospital Board and management was taken over by the Board of Management for Glasgow and District Children's Hospitals, which formally assumed direction at that meeting.

The new board of management was responsible for the Children's Home Hospital, Strathblane, as well as for Yorkhill and the country branch. Later they were joined by a new partner, the Queen Mother's Hospital, which opened on Yorkhill in 1964. The group then became known as Yorkhill Children's and Maternity Hospitals, and its board of management is responsible for both the 'Sick Kids' and the 'Queen Mum's' – to give them their less formal titles – and for Drumchapel Hospital for geriatric patients.

It was 'with some regret' that the directors of the voluntary hospital submitted their last annual report. 'The passing of the voluntary hospitals and their great tradition of service must be viewed by many with mixed feelings,' stated the report. The board had long argued in favour of retaining the voluntary hospitals within the proposed national system; and among the directors there was much disappointment that whereas English teaching hospitals had been allowed to retain their endowment funds and had independent boards of management directly responsible to the Ministry of Health, no such provision had been made for Scotland.

Yorkhill's endowment funds were considerable. Reluctant at all times to allow expenditure to eat into capital, the board had long been noted for thrift rather than extravagance; and post-war building restrictions would in any case have prevented an expansionist policy. Now, under the National Health Act, Yorkhill's endowments, along with those of the other former voluntary hospitals, were examined by an Endowments Commission charged with submitting schemes for their use to the Secretary of State for Scotland. Some of Yorkhill's money was used for the benefit of other hospitals in more urgent financial need; but the board retained control over substantial amounts of the endowment funds, including all post-1948 endowments, and from this source was financed much of the energetic building programme that followed the removal of post-war restrictions.

Despite the initial fears, the hospital has continued to flourish in the years since 1948 – which have indeed been the ones of the most rapid and remarkable medical advances of its history – and the break with the past was less sharp than some had perhaps expected. Significantly, perhaps, the seal of the old hospital, a miniature of Raphael's Sistine Madonna, was adopted by the new board (despite the Rothesay Herald's warning that since the design was not armorial it was outside his jurisdiction to protect it from pirates). In other ways, too, there was continuity with the past. Of the 18 members of the new board eight had served on the old one – that is, a quarter of the original board. Robert Barclay's successor, Sir Thomas Dunlop, continued as chairman of the new board; and Mr Andrew R. Templeton, honorary treasurer of the old board since 1943, became deputy chairman of the new board and convener of its finance committee.

The new board, unlike the old one, included members of the hospital medical staff – Professor Stanley Graham, Matthew White, Dr George Montgomery, pathologist and Gardiner lecturer, and Dr Findlay Ford, physician, were among its original members. Meetings were also attended by the hospital matron and the group secretary.

Since 1948 the board has had three chairmen: Sir Thomas Dunlop (till 1957), Mrs Alexander MacLellan (1957 to 1968), and Mr Richard H. Barclay (from 1968).

Thomas Dunlop, who was a well-known Glasgow shipowner and insurance broker, had a shorter association with Yorkhill than his

Sir Thomas Dunlop

Mrs Alexander MacLellan

*Mr Richard Barclay,
chairman of the Board.*

predecessor, Robert Barclay; but the task is said to have been close to his heart and he brought to the office of chairman a vast experience in public service. The Merchants' House and the Fine Art Institute were among the Glasgow institutions which he served, and he was a member of public bodies ranging from the Licensing Appeal Court to the Clyde Navigation Trust – as well as being at one time consul in Glasgow for Serbia, Croatia, and Slovenia, and later for Paraguay. He was also a well-known yachtsman and former vice-commodore of the Royal Clyde Yacht Club.

His successor, Mrs Alexander MacLellan, brought to her task a long record of hospital service and in particular a valuable knowledge of the ways of children's hospitals. It was in the early 1920s that Mrs MacLellan joined the ladies' committee of Strathblane Children's Home Hospital, with which she has maintained an active connection to this day; and through her late husband, a Yorkhill director for many years, she was well acquainted with the children's hospital before she herself joined the board.

Mr Richard Barclay, the present chairman, also has a long association with the hospital reaching back well beyond his first formal connection with it. Mr Barclay, who joined the board in 1955, is the son of Robert Barclay, who served the hospital as honorary secretary and later also as chairman for so many years. Like his father, Mr Barclay has a professional link with the hospital in its earliest years. The old firm of Andrew Macgeorge and later of Robert Barclay, so closely bound up with the foundation and subsequent growth of the hospital, merged in the 1920s with another city firm of solicitors to become Baird Smith, Barclay and Muirhead; and later this firm itself amalgamated with Maclay, Murray and Spens, in which Mr Richard Barclay is now a partner.

The three post-war chairmen have one thing in common. Each has held office during a critically important phase in the hospital's history: Dunlop during the first years of nationalisation and the beginning of the dramatic growth which followed the restrictions of war-time and of post-war austerity; Mrs MacLellan during the time when the decision was taken to build the hospital anew; and Mr Barclay – like his father before him – during the building and opening of a new hospital at Yorkhill.

Medical administration, like medicine itself, has grown more complex in these years. In this field, too, a certain continuity was

Mr James Methven

Dr Hugh Park

Mr Robert Dunlop

preserved on nationalisation. Mr James Methven, secretary of the hospital since 1931 – except for break for war service when his yorkhill duties were carried out by Miss Hannah Robertson – became secretary of the new group, and later played a vital part in the arrangements for the evacuation of the hospital to Oakbank. Campbell Suttie continued as medical superintendent. These two were the officers directly responsible to the board of management for the administration of the hospital.

Campbell Suttie was succeeded in 1953 by Dr R. O. Cairns; and since 1964 the group medical superintendent has been Dr Hugh Park, formerly deputy area medical superintendent of North and South Ayrshire Hospitals, who also played a leading part in the migration to Oakbank in 1964 and in the recent return journey to Yorkhill. When Mr Methven retired in 1968 he was succeeded by the present group secretary, Mr Robert Dunlop.

Chapter 20

PAEDIATRICIANS' PROGRESS

IN 1947, when Professor Stanley Graham followed Geoffrey Fleming to the Chair of Child Health, paediatrics was coming to be accepted as a 'respectable' and indeed major division of medicine. Twenty years before, when Leonard Findlay was in his heyday at Yorkhill and Professor Graham was his assistant, the Samson Gemmell Chair had been the only one of its kind in the United Kingdom. Now, in 1947 – which was also, incidentally, the year of Findlay's death – almost every university in the country had a Chair of child health or was taking steps to establish one.

The early, pioneering days were past. Unlike Leonard Findlay, who worked for a time at the Western Infirmary in adult medicine, Professor Graham and his successor, Professor James Hutchison, brought to their posts many years of full-time experience in paediatrics.

Professor Graham, the son of a Scottish doctor who had emigrated to Canada, graduated in 1916 from Toronto University – which later, in his professorial years, honoured him with an LL.D. He joined the Yorkhill staff in 1923 as assistant to Leonard Findlay – and looks back still with vivid enjoyment to the 'stimulating, crazy mornings' of his chief's ward rounds. In 1931 he himself was placed in charge of wards and became Gow lecturer, occupying this post until 1947. During this period he undertook major research into the scientific basis of infant feeding and also became an expert on hypocalcaemia and on problems of acid/base balance. In his 14 years as Samson Gemmell Professor he was responsible for many advances at Yorkhill – and in particular bore the burden of increased teaching commitments in

154

Professor Stanley Graham   *Professor James Hutchison*

inadequate surroundings; and in 1955 he became president of the British Paediatric Association.

Professor Graham is remembered at Yorkhill for his personal charm as well as for his professional stature. He is remembered, too, as an excellent teacher both in the lecture room and in the ward. 'Younger colleagues,' recalls one of them, 'soon discovered that assertions made without evidence to support them would inevitably result in their being sent off to the library, or even the laboratory, with instructions to collect the necessary evidence.'

His private consulting practice must have been one of the largest in the country – not surprisingly, since he was 'a superb clinician whose advice the family doctors greatly valued'. 'I think he was happiest when he ran a busy consulting practice combined with hospital work and research,' comments Professor Hutchison. 'When he became a full-time university professor he missed the challenges of private practice more than some others have done. Furthermore, he was denied the chance of seeing a modern, properly equipped teaching and research department built during his tenure of the Chair. As has happened to so many others, he saw such a department come to his successor – largely through the efforts which he himself had exerted during his 14 years in the Chair.'

Professor Graham and his wife – theirs was one of a number of Yorkhill marriages, for in the 1920s Mrs Graham was a research scholar and assistant physician at the hospital – now live in retirement in Callander.

Professor James Hutchison, who succeeded Professor Graham as Gow lecturer in 1947 and as Samson Gemmell Professor in 1961, has been a paediatrician all his senior professional life. After graduating from Glasgow University in 1934 he became a Yorkhill houseman and soon afterwards, flying in the face of some weighty warnings about the inexpediency of careers in paediatrics, decided to devote his work to this field. In 1938, shortly after his M.D. thesis had won him the Bellahouston gold medal at Glasgow University, he became visiting assistant physican in Professor Graham's unit; and it was to Yorkhill that he returned after being awarded an O.B.E. on war service to become Gow lecturer in the re-alignment that followed Geoffrey Fleming's retiral. As Samson Gemmell Professor since 1961 he, too, has been associated with many major advances at Yorkhill including the establishment of the social paediatric unit, and the building of the present up-to-date university department of child health. His researches have included work on tuberculosis, thyroid disorders, methods of resuscitating newborn infants, and respiratory diseases in the newborn baby. He is the author of a widely used textbook, *Practical Paediatric Problems*. In 1971 he was awarded the C.B.E.

During the quarter of a century in which Professor Graham and Professor Hutchison have successively occupied the Gemmell Chair, great changes have taken place at Yorkhill – some of them pioneered in Glasgow, others forming part of a more general pattern. These years have seen more specialisation; more medical teamwork; more preventive paediatrics; more research; and both the development of such established fields as biochemistry and pathology and the emergence of newer ones, from child psychiatry to cytogenetics. In response to these greater demands the university department of child health has also grown, and in addition to the occupant of the Gemmell Chair now includes a titular professor associated with the hospital, Professor Gavin Arneil.

The entire pattern of child health has changed in those years. Such old, persistent ailments as rickets and scurvy have now, thanks to preventive medicine, ceased to be a problem. Largely vanquished, too, thanks to the rapid development of new antimicrobial drugs, are such former deadly enemies as pneumonia, cerebrospinal meningitis, tuberculosis, osteomyelitis, and gastroenteritis. Tuberculosis, in some of its forms at least, has been on the decline for several decades; and Yorkhill had an important role to play in its further retreat in Glasgow. Shortly after the war the hospital became one of the few in Scotland selected by the Medical Research Council for streptomycin tests on tuberculous patients, and the use of B.C.G. vaccination for newborn babies was pioneered in Glasgow – the first city in Britain to use it, under the influence of Yorkhill.

Penicillin, first introduced at Yorkhill in 1944 – when 'each case has been under constant bacteriological supervision' – continued to be pitted against the previously lethal powers of streptococcal disease and consequently rheumatic heart disease. In the post-war years, too, antibiotics along with advances in biochemistry enabled doctors to come to grips with infantile gastroenteritis. The 1940s had seen an alarming increase in the incidence of this disease – and of dysenteric infections generally – until it became the commonest cause of death in young children. 'No satisfactory cause or cure has so far been discovered,' wrote the Yorkhill pathologist, Dr Katherine Guthrie, in the epidemic year of 1944, when 166 cases were treated in the hospital. Now, however, in the words of Professor Hutchison, 'increasing understanding from research into body water and electrolytes, using new micromethods and antibiotics, has resulted in a rapid fall in the deaths from gastroenteritis – and has also permitted the paediatric surgeons to undertake more safely major operations upon many congenital anomalies of the newborn which had previously been irremediable.'

More than half Yorkhill's patients are under the age of five; and the continuous downward trend in the average age of patients, which dates back to the hospital's Garnethill days, has now reached its logical conclusion in the development of neonatal medicine. 'At last the paediatrician and the obstetrician have learned to work together', comments Professor Hutchison, 'and the future of the ill newborn baby has been transformed by the researches and intensive type of care now undertaken by the modern whole-time, scientifically-orientated paediatrician.' Of immense significance for the children's hospital was the opening of the Queen Mother's Hospital on what had previously been the home battleground of Yorkhill's combined nurses' and doctors' hockey team. The first baby was born at the

Mr Andrew Laird

Mr Wallace Dennison

Mr Sam Davidson

Queen Mother's Hospital in January 1964 – and the first baby to be transferred from the new hospital to Yorkhill was admitted in the same month. A link bridge re-unites the re-built children's hospital with the Queen Mother's, and for the first time the former includes accommodation for mothers – a state of affairs which would have won the hearty approval of James Nicoll.

★   ★   ★

Paediatric surgery has also made immense strides since the war, and Yorkhill has been closely associated with a number of major advances. During the war leadership in this field had passed to the United States, although at Yorkhill Matthew White continued such pioneering as was possible under the circumstances, performing the first successful operation in the world for large-bowel atresia (blockage caused by developmental anomaly). Now, in the post-war years, the torch – to use Matthew White's own term – was passed back to the United Kingdom; and at Yorkhill the pioneering tradition of Alexander MacLennan was carried on by White and his successor, Mr Wallace Dennison, and by such other leading surgeons as Mr Andrew Laird and, later, Mr Sam Davidson, Mr John Bentley and Mr Dan Young. The post-war tendency – fostered by White – for more of the hospital's surgeons to abandon work in the general hospitals in favour of Yorkhill encouraged progress in this field. Members of the present surgical staff whose hospital work had been entirely at Yorkhill since that period include Mr Dennison (who was a house surgeon in 1932 and joined the visiting staff in 1936) and Mr Stewart Mann.

Progress in the post-war years ranged over many fields of paediatric surgery. Matthew White was responsible for pioneering work in chest surgery; and together he and Mr Dennison wrote the first undergraduate textbook in English paediatric surgery. Mr Andrew Laird – like his old chief, Alexander MacLennan – was closely interested in the development of orthopaedic work and devised two operations for the treatment of club foot. He also undertook much important work in plastic surgery, and introduced a plastic operation – it became known as Laird's operation – for the correction of hypospadias, a defect of the lower urinary tract. Pioneering work was also done in the treatment of cleft palates. After Dunkirk

159

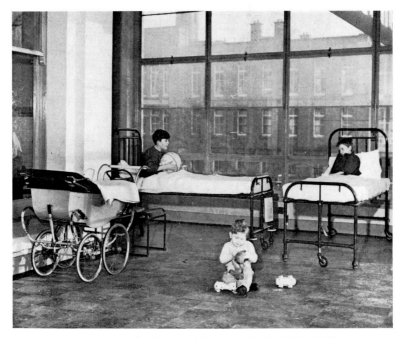

Passing the time in one of the wards in the old Yorkhill.

dentists and doctors had learned to work together in the treatment of gunshot wounds in the jaw, and this co-operation was continued in civilian life. At Yorkhill Dr C. Kerr McNeil, emeritus reader in oral orthopaedics at Glasgow University, introduced the oral orthopaedic treatment of cleft palates – moulding the jaw in order to give the surgeons a good, bony foundation on which to work. At a time when some children with cleft palates were considered mentally defective Dr McNeil was among those who established that impaired hearing was in fact responsible for this impression. There followed a new approach to cleft palate treatment, combining the work of specialists in ear, nose, and throat surgery, audiology, speech therapy, and oral orthopaedics.

The development of antibiotics, the availability of blood plasma, and progress in anaesthetics have permitted major advances in many other branches of paediatric surgery. The advance of anaesthetics far beyond the rag-and-bottle days to a sophisticated division of anaesthesia has allowed surgeons to undertake with confidence operations lasting for three or four hours. This has enormously increased the scope for operations on young babies and together with advances in surgical technique has resulted in, for example, a very high survival rate for children operated on for severe cases of spina bifida in the early hours of life.

'Much of the drama has been in neonatal surgery,' comments Mr Wallace Dennison, who has been Barclay lecturer in paediatric surgery since 1953. In the early 1950s great advances in neonatal surgery were being pioneered south of the Border, and Yorkhill became associated with these glamorous advances while still undertaking a heavy load of bread-and-butter surgery. In 1960, with between 400 and 500 patients being admitted monthly to the surgical wards of the hospital, it was noted that over the previous decade there had been a steady increase in neonatal surgical emergency cases until they became half as common as acute appendicitis. 'Yorkhill is now one of the busiest children's hospitals in the United Kingdom', stated a hospital memorandum of that year. 'In addition to the routine and emergency surgery, we are attempting to cope with the neonatal and cardiac problems which are being dealt with in such specialised hospitals as Great Ormond Street.'

Like neonatal surgery, orthopaedics has emerged as a distinct specialisation; and just as the one would have delighted James Nicoll, so the other would have greatly gratified Alexander MacLennan, who advocated it in the 1920s. In 1956 Mr Noel Blockey became the hospital's first consultant orthopaedic surgeon, and the Barclay lectureship was divided into its constituent parts, Mr Blockey becoming Barclay lecturer in orthopaedics. Mr Duncan Macpherson is his assistant.

The development of orthopaedic surgery, with much work being done in the later treatment of spina bifida children, has been accompanied by the growth of such related fields as physiotherapy and the manufacture of surgical appliances. The appliances department – the successor to the splint department so efficiently built up by Miss Sophia Muirhead between the wars – has won a reputation for ingenuity combined with inspired simplicity of design. Their inventions include the Yorkhill chair – now used in other hospitals and other countries – which was put together from such basic components as a child's car seat, pram wheels, and castors. Another notable success is the Yorkhill sledge – a wheeled bogie for paraplegic children, who are often extremely active before being old enough to use a wheel-

L

chair. One reckless Yorkhill sledger collided so often with the furniture that a crash helmet had to be made for him.

★   ★   ★

Such specialities as haematology and cytogenetics, unheard of in Leonard Findlay's day, now play a vital part at Yorkhill, a practical application of the latter being genetic counselling – assessing the likelihood of, say, a mother bearing a second mongol child.

Important contributions to the treatment of diseases of the central nervous system have been made by Dr Robert Shanks, who became consultant paediatrician in charge of wards in 1961 and has pioneered and developed the E.E.G. (electro-encephalography) services of the hospital. As physician-superintendent of East Park Home for handicapped children he helped to pioneer the treatment and assessment of all types of physical and mental handicap. The addition to the new hospital of a child assessment unit – the gift of the Fraser Foundation – is expected to encourage further developments in paediatric neurology.

From small beginnings the hospital's cardiac services were developed in the 1960s by Dr Eric Coleman, and today Yorkhill has one of the finest and busiest such departments in the country; the new hospital also accommodates the team of paediatric heart surgeons hitherto based on Mearnskirk. Paediatric nephrology and paediatric endocrinology are among other emergent specialisations, and Professor Gavin Arneil and Dr William Hamilton have been associated with important developments in these fields.

Older specialisations have also grown in importance and assumed new functions. On Campbell Suttie's retirement in 1953 the posts of medical superintendent and radiologist were separated, with resultant benefits. Dr Simon Rawson was made head of the X-ray department and Yorkhill now has three radiologists. Under Dr George Montgomery and his successor as Gardiner lecturer, Dr Alistair MacDonald, the work of the pathology department has grown greatly, even if the consequent expansion has meant the eviction of Yorkhill's badminton players from the pathology museum. And under Dr Ellis Wilson and his successor, Dr Robert Logan, the biochemistry department continued to grow in the post-war years and has now extended its services to provide a screening function for the

Dr Ellis Wilson　　　　　　*Mr Noel Blockey*

Dr Robert Shanks

newborn. Dr Wilson, who early in his career worked for the All-India Institute of Hygiene and Public Health, became Yorkhill biochemist and university lecturer in biochemistry in the late 1930s; and like his ebullient predecessor, Noah Morris, he was both an outstanding Yorkhill personality and a leading biochemist. In the 1950s the laboratory on the roof of Ward 4 was the scene of his pioneering work in methods associated with the study of peptides, the compounds formed by the union of amino-acids. 'This overcrowded laboratory,' recalls Professor Arneil, 'became a centre for the study of renal problems – and also the home of a multitude of white rats which were fed daily by gastric tube.'

Specialised clinics, a long-established part of the hospital's work, continue to play their part. When the West Graham Street dispensary was closed in 1953 – and with it a chapter of Cowcaddens history – a new temporary out-patient department was opened at Yorkhill, providing clinics in medical and surgical diseases, skin diseases, eye diseases, dental diseases, and diseases of ear, nose, and throat. An important departure in more recent years was the establishment of a deafness clinic.

With the growth of specialisation, teamwork has become more and more essential. Seldom nowadays is a child treated by one doctor only, and the hospital's medical administration has an important part to play balancing and reconciling the various resources. It is in this field that the new child assessment unit will play a major part. As well as teamwork among paediatricians there has also been co-operation with specialists who work with all age groups, such as plastic surgeons and urologists. New links have been forged not only with the obstetrician but the geriatrician, and a geriatric unit is now attached to the hospital's Drumchapel branch. The two medical specialisations to be based on age have, in fact, much in common. Co-operation with the neighbouring counties has also grown and each one now has at least one consultant paediatrician in close contact with Yorkhill.

'Somewhat belatedly,' notes Professor Hutchison, 'the paediatrician has developed a real interest in disease prevention, normal and abnormal growth and development, and the co-ordination care of the handicapped child.' When a child welfare department was established in 1946, in association with the university and Glasgow Corporation, it was intended as 'a first step towards the co-ordination

164

between preventive medicine, nutrition, child care, and the clinical aspects of paediatrics'. A logical development of this trend was child psychiatry, and in 1954 Dr Frederick Stone was appointed consultant

Dr Frederick Stone   *Mr Dan Young*

in this subject. In the following year the department of child psychiatry was opened at 70 University Avenue – Campbell Suttie's old home – and later came the opening of a day centre at Woodlands Terrace, where therapy could be combined with education or nursery school activities. Dr Stones' department is now housed in the new hospital.

★   ★   ★

The growth of paediatric work has confounded some post-war predictions. The development of modern obstetrics, the growth of welfare services, and the decline of infectious diseases led many optimists to suppose that the need for paediatric services would decline. 'But in fact the reverse has happened,' points out Dr Hugh Park, the hospital's medical superintendent. 'These developments mean that children who in earlier times would have died in early infancy now survive. These are children without the best health prospects, but they are thus more likely to be admitted to a paediatric unit.'

A case in point is spina bifida. Neonatal surgical techniques have led to the survival of many more of these children after birth – with varying levels of handicap which require regular attention from orthopaedic surgeons and other specialists. At the same time Yorkhill now treats many children with congenital abnormalities – such as heart disease – who would at one time never have been admitted to the wards because nothing could have been done for them.

It was the enormous and shocking proportions of Victorian infantile mortality that spurred the hospital's founders to action more than a century ago. The rate has declined dramatically since the Second World War, here as elsewhere; but Glasgow still remains distressingly near the top of the table. An important cause of this is the high proportion of large families in the city – a quarter of all the babies born in Glasgow are the fourth or subsequent children of their families, and for them the risk of neonatal or perinatal death is greater, especially if the births have followed in fairly quick succession. The mothers of these large families are often the ones least in a position to seek the ante-natal care which could reduce the death rate.

While many old enemies have been almost banished as the result of antibiotics and preventive medicine, certain other diseases have gained prominence. Malignant diseases, including leukaemia and kidney tumours, are much more common than before the war. Yorkhill is now a Medical Research Council centre for the treatment of malignant disease, and Professor Hutchison is chairman of the M.R.C. working party on childhood leukaemia.

Malignant diseases and accidents now account for most of the deaths of children over the age of one, although of course they affect all age groups. Accidents in the home outnumber even those in the streets, and, as with adults, poisoning cases have greatly increased. Bizarre examples of the latter include 11 girls who made pea soup from laburnum peas; and a boy who made a habit of standing on snakes – and missed.

But not all Yorkhill's patients can be neatly slotted into medical and surgical classifications. Even in an age of cytogenetics the occasional chamber pot has to be dislodged from the head of some unfortunate child. And mothers have been known to arrive at the hospital with an infant under one arm and a sewing machine under the other, seeking the skill of a surgeon to part the one from the other.

Chapter 21

RESEARCH

RESEARCH at Yorkhill has come a long way since puzzled dogs were confined in barrels to further Leonard Findlay's investigations into the cause of rickets. After the war the small roof-top laboratories in the old Yorkhill buildings became the scene of much modern and sophisticated research.

In Glasgow, as elsewhere, the provision of adequate research accommodation did not immediately follow the creation of a Chair of child health; and Professor Hutchison comments that 'it is one of the ironies of life that the modern academic department now on the Yorkhill site with its two large research laboratories was completed only after the old hospital was found to be so dangerous in structure as to necessitate its complete evacuation'. Since 1964, however, the child health department has had five small laboratories in the new Queen Mother's hospital. The staff of the department has also grown and now, in addition to the Samson Gemmell and titular professors, has three senior lecturers, three lecturers, and three National Health Service consultants. One of the senior lecturers, Dr Malcolm Ferguson-Smith, is a geneticist with an international reputation. Another member of the department, Dr Gerald Richards, leads the social research group which cooperates closely with Glasgow Corporation health department, and has its headquarters in their building. Research grants and finances have also been obtained from many other sources, including the Children's Research Fund, the Cystic Fibrosis Research Foundation, the Scottish Hospitals Endowments Research Trust, and the Secretary of State for Scotland.

Research at Yorkhill is not confined to the department of child

This drawing of Yorkhill was made in the 1950s.

health but has also increased in N.H.S.-financed departments. The haematology department, for example, undertakes intensive research into leukaemia, led by Dr Michael Willoughby and supported by the Medical Research Council. Research is also being carried out in nephrology, endocrinology, nutrition, cardiology, gastroenterology, and neonatology.

Many research projects – like much clinical work – are now the work of teams which, in addition to paediatricians, geneticists, or epidemiologists, include biochemists, psychologists, physicists, and even engineers. Dieticians are among members of the team investigating cystic fibrosis. One of the biggest research projects in which

168

Yorkhill plays a part is the International Collaborative Study of Kidney Disease in Children, of which Professor Arneil is the British director.

'All this,' comments Professor Hutchison, 'is a far cry from my early days in paediatrics when a few young men worked, unassisted by science graduates and trained technicians, for about £250 a year on research projects which had to be undertaken in the hours which busy service commitments left free.'

Professor Gavin Arneil

But some themes recur in the history of Yorkhill. Rickets has again recently been the subject of research – though with methods far removed from Leonard Findlay's canine experiments of 40 years before. This disease, so notoriously prevalent in Glasgow in the early years of the hospital's history, has declined rapidly from the mid-1920s and was given a final push towards oblivion when vitamin D was added to national dried milk during the war. This was more palatable than cod-liver oil – which had languished by the gallon on the shelves of welfare clinics or on the shelf at home or had been, if the worst came to the worst, spat out. Between 1952 and 1958 only two cases of rickets were seen at the hospital annually – a happy contrast with 1918 when Sister Elinor was hard put to it to find enough non-rachitic children at the dispensary to be research controls. Complications associated with overdoses of vitamin D led, however, to smaller amounts being added to national dried milk and cereals – and rickets re-appeared in Glasgow infants. Contrary to a widespread belief, 90 per cent of these children were of Scottish and not immigrant descent. In 1964 the hospital treated 24 cases of gross rickets; and after consultations with Glasgow Corporation a survey, led by Professor Arneil, was made of children in Bridgeton, Springburn, and the Gorbals. Cases of active gross rickets were found to be latent in the population, making it clear that 'a problem of malnutrition existed in Glasgow'. A survey of 4000 Scottish children followed; various dietary and other recommendations were made, and it was observed that 'cod-liver oil should be honourably retired' and that 'obstetricians should stop urging reluctant mothers to breast feed in hospital when they tend to stop as soon as they go home. This simply leads to the habit of ignoring medical advice.'

Bottled milk, too, has again become the subject of research at contemporary Yorkhill. Long after its traditional dangers had been removed by pasteurisation, atomic bomb testing posed a new problem – the absorption of radio-active strontium. The problem was twofold – how to reduce the intake, and how to remove it afterwards. Flinging out the old A.R.P. stirrup pumps, relics of a vanished pre-atomic age, Professor Arneil and his researchers took over the castellated outhouse on the roof of ward 12 and turned it into a highly sophisticated laboratory. A metabolic room was constructed for the radio-biological monitoring of strontium metabolism in children. This Yorkhill team of clinicians and pathologists, together with Dr J. M. A. Lenihan of the Regional Department of Clinical Physics and Bio-engineering, were responsible for the great bulk of United Kingdom research into this problem in children.

★ ★ ★

The increasing complexity of modern medicine is reflected in the heavier undergraduate and post-graduate teaching commitments of the hospital's medical staff. Senior members of the staff also devote time to medical affairs outside the hospital, such as government, college, and university committees. Professor Hutchison is at present

Dean of the Faculty of Medicine at Glasgow University and chairman of the Standing Medical Advisory Committee in the Scottish Home and Health Department; he is also an examiner in adult medicine for membership of the Royal College of Physicians of London – an unusual compliment to a paediatrician. He and his two immediate predecessors have been presidents of the Royal College of Physicians and Surgeons of Glasgow, and all four Samson Gemmell professors have been presidents of the British Paediatric Association. It was at Yorkhill that the European Society for Paediatric Nephrology was founded in 1967, with 24 countries represented. The hospital's paediatric surgeons have been active in the Scottish Association of Paediatric Surgeons, formed in 1948, and later in the British Association of Paediatric Surgeons which developed from it. When the association held their annual meeting in Holland in 1964 they were without a president; and Mr Wallace Dennison was elected to this office at an extraordinary general meeting, which certainly lived up to its name – it was held in the luggage van of a train travelling between Rotterdam and Eindhoven. He is also an honorary Fellow – there are only 27 in the world – of the American Academy of Pediatrics.

In Leonard Findlay's day the world came to Yorkhill; it still does, but now the traffic is two-way. International conferences have been attended, overseas hospitals visited, and lectures given in countries ranging from Thailand to Nigeria, and Mexico to the Sudan.

Former post-war members of the Yorkhill staff have since occupied important posts at home and overseas. Dr Findlay Ford, formerly first assistant to Professor Graham, left Yorkhill for the Chair of Paediatrics in Capetown, where his work did much to raise the status of South African paediatrics. Professor George Montgomery, of the Chair of Pathology at Edinburgh University, was once Gardiner lecturer and Yorkhill pathologist. Dr Patrick McArthur, an outstanding Yorkhill physician of the post-war period, is paediatric consultant to the Northern Regional Hospital Board.

Even full-time paediatricians, however, are fortunately not paediatricians for 24 hours a day. No surgeons now hover above the hospital in Gypsy Moths, as Matthew White once did; but Mr Andrew Laird's dexterity in making models to decorate his wards at Christmas earned him the title of 'the plaster king of Yorkhill' and one of his ambitions in retirement is, he says, to build a plaster Taj

*Distant prospect of
Gilmorehill from the
entrance to Yorkhill in
the mid-1960s.*

The new university department of child health at Yorkhill.

Mahal. Scottish country dancing is among Professor Hutchison's accomplishments, and he also takes part in the annual golf match between Glasgow and Aberdeen universities. All-round sportsmen include Professor Arneil, who has frequently played for Yorkhill against all-comers in that savage inter-hospital sport, mixed hockey. Dr Shanks is an accomplished pianist. Mr Mann is an expert on surgical history and not least on the work of James Nicoll at the children's dispensary. He has also in recent years become an accomplished Gaelic scholar. Dr Ellis Wilson, though he was noted for his frugal lunching in his room at Yorkhill, is an expert on food and wine; and together with several colleagues imported barrels of wine from France and held bottling parties in the kitchen of his house – with as many as 700 bottles a time being laid down for the future.

Amid all the clinical seriousness and scientific endeavour, the hospital itself has been the scene of lighthearted episodes. The post-war annals of Yorkhill's history include a kidnapping raid on the conservatory, led by an Austrian research assistant and resulting in the abduction of the marble baby from its resting place beside the fountain. The search party eventually gave up; and years later the baby turned up in the basement.

The inevitable domestic calamities – which date back to the day the boiler burst on Garnethill – continue to occur from time to time. A minor explosion in one of the laboratories once, as the board minutes put it, 'rendered unwearable' a pair of trousers belonging to one of the technicians. More serious was the total breakdown of Yorkhill's telephone system on a nerve-wracking day in November 1967, when communications with the outside world had to be maintained by police wireless trucks.

Long ago on Garnethill the matron, Julia Simpson, was photographed in the company of 'one of her temporary charges' – a lion cub. In recent years, too, the hospital has had its animal visitors. Escaped monkeys from the nearby Kelvin Hall once cleverly dodged their pursuers on one of the Yorkhill roofs and as a final insult plundered food from a pantry. More popular was the pet pigeon brought to the hospital with a broken wing – Mr Laird put it in splints and a case sheet was made out.

Even more famous than Mr Laird's pigeon, and attracting attention in the press, was Carmen, a patient of Professor Arneil's. Called to the telephone one Christmas at Yorkhill, Professor (then

Dr) Arneil was astonished to find himself being asked to treat a chimpanzee, the star of a performing troupe in the Kelvin Hall circus. Amid the laughter of his colleagues he set off down the hill to find five chimpanzees jumping up and down and a sixth, Carmen, lying still. 'A glance at the pattern of breathing spelt the diagnosis of pneumonia,' recalls Professor Arneil, 'but an attempt at using a stethoscope was like listening to a coconut mat while dust was being shaken out.' To avoid cross-infection Carmen was given the ladies' dressing room in the Kelvin Hall as an isolation ward. Placed under an oxygen tent she settled down on her back with her legs crossed. Terramycin, reports Professor Arneil, was prescribed but there were fears that tuberculosis – apparently common in chimpanzees – might be underlying; and so late (and unofficially) one evening Carmen, disguised in a jacket and cap, was driven to Yorkhill's X-ray department. After the X-ray, while her trainer chatted to Dr Rawson and Dr Arneil, Carmen opened the door and departed unnoticed into the corridor until 'the anguished yell of a night sister disappearing down the corridor brought us all back to our senses.' By the time the porter came to investigate, Carmen, in hat and jacket, was on her way back to the Kelvin Hall. She duly made a welcome re-appearance in the chimpanzee orchestra.

Chapter 22

NURSING

THE Victorian parents who padded into Mrs Harbin's wards in their stocking soles, in the days when boots were banned, would have been astonished at the behaviour of their counterparts at Yorkhill today. Parents are now encouraged to participate in the care of the patients; mothers come and go, bathing and feeding their off-spring, and fathers are sometimes to be seen brushing their children's teeth.

Paediatric progress at Yorkhill has not been merely a matter of impersonal scientific advances. 'The noisy, cheerful atmosphere of the wards,' comments one physician, 'reflects a new appreciation of the emotional needs and disturbances of children.' Gone for good are the days when patients were obliged to wear lace-edged collars over their scarlet bedjackets when the matron made her daily ward round. (Several such relics of a long-vanished past caused initial puzzlement when they were discovered in a linen cupboard during the war.) Gone, too, are the days when diversionary trolleyloads of fruit and milk and biscuits had to be hastily trundled into the wards when visiting hour was over; in the 1950s, on the initiative of Professor Stanley Graham, visiting hours were gradually extended, and for a number of years now they have been unrestricted.

Under the two post-war matrons, Miss Ruth Clarkson and her successor, Miss Olive Hulme, much has changed in the day-to-day lives not only of patients but of nurses. Both matrons, too, have held their posts during critical periods of the hospital's nursing history: Miss Clarkson during the difficulties of wartime and during the nursing shortage which continued into the post-war period; Miss

Miss Ruth Clarkson   *Miss Olive Hulme*

Nurses at a lecture in the late 1950s.

Hulme during the emergency evacuation to Oakbank Hospital and the exigencies of life there.

Miss Clarkson, who succeeded Miss Robinson in 1941, was Yorkhill's matron for 20 years, sharing with the first matron, Mrs Harbin, the record for length of service at this post; and in both cases the contribution to the hospital was considerable. Just as many of her medical colleagues at post-war Yorkhill had been paediatricians for most of their careers, so Miss Clarkson had from the outset specialised in paediatric nursing, having trained at Great Ormond Street Hospital in London. Her association with, and interest in, paediatrics dates back further, for her father was R. D. Clarkson, founder of the first colony providing life care for mentally defective children in Scotland and friend of John Thomson of Edinburgh and of Leonard Findlay. Miss Clarkson's mother, too, was a nurse – 'I'm a purely hospital product,' she adds, 'for my father and mother met when they were working at the Royal Hospital for Sick Children, Edinburgh.'

A significant and welcome change during Miss Clarkson's day was that after the coming of the National Health Service the hospital matron was freed from her traditional household responsibilities and allowed to devote her energies exclusively to nursing administration. Hitherto, matrons from Mrs Harbin onwards had been responsible for the household stores, and when Miss Clarkson first came to Yorkhill she 'could have told you to the last cake of soap how much was used in the wards'. At the same time, with the creation of a new board of management, provision was made for the matron to attend board meetings, Miss Clarkson becoming the first to do so. Among important advances which she herself initiated was the introduction of a preliminary training course for nurses. Until then they had gone straight into the wards.

Significant changes in paediatric nurses' training, which was broadened to include experience outside the hospital, have come about during the period since Miss Olive Hulme, the present matron, succeeded Miss Clarkson in 1961. Miss Hulme is the first matron of the hospital to have been trained at Yorkhill herself – her first matron was Miss Robinson – and she has also worked there as a ward Sister, after undergoing her general and midwifery training. When she returned to Yorkhill in 1961 – after a period as assistant matron at the Royal Hospital for Sick Children, Edinburgh – Miss

The nurses' sitting-room in the late 1950s.

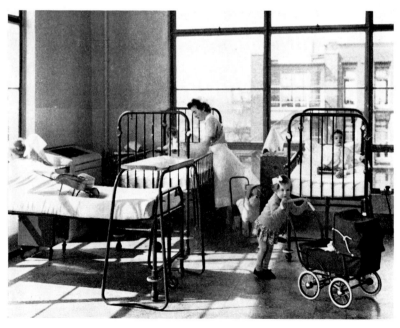

A ward scene in the late 1950s.

Mrs Alexander MacLellan on a visit to the wards during her term of office as chairman. With her is Mr Noel Blockey, Barclay lecturer in orthopaedic surgery.

Hulme was hardly to know that in only a few years her headquarters would be several miles from Yorkhill. She played a leading part in the emergency evacuation to Oakbank, for which she was later awarded an M.B.E.

Medical advances have resulted not only in the inevitable changes in the nurses' training curriculum but also in fundamental changes in the nature of paediatric nursing itself. Few patients now receive the prolonged conservative treatment once given to, for example, children suffering from malnutrition; and as treatment has become quicker and more dramatic in its effects children have tended to return home sooner or to move on to the Drumchapel branch. With this rapid turn-over in the wards, nurses nowadays seldom see their patients fully recovered. The greater part played by parents in the care of patients has also brought about changes in the rôle of the nurses. 'The paediatric nurse is no longer a mother-substitute in the way she used to be,' comments Miss Hulme. 'She has to learn to sit back at times and let the children belong to the mother.'

Outside the wards, too, nursing life has changed in many ways; and the days are gone when nurses dared not venture outside the nurses' home without their hats. Improvements have been made, too, in their living and recreational quarters. During Mrs MacLellan's chairmanship, and with her close interest and assistance, a major refurbishing took place – with inspiration for the colour scheme of the nurses' sitting room being drawn from Daly's tearoom in Sauchiehall Street. The sitting room and its golden pillars have now turned to dust, but previous generations of nurses might envy the new flatlets in Yorkhill Court, the staff residential quarters beside the new hospital. These accommodate 127 nurses, four to a flat. Nowadays there is no curfew – which would have astounded Mrs Harbin – but when the flats were first occupied it was noticed that returning nurses sometimes preferred to enter the building in the traditional way, through the windows.

Chapter 23

THE GREAT MIGRATION

THE Oakbank interlude – if that term does not sound too idyllic – is an odd and isolated chapter in the hospital's history, but one with more than its share of drama. It was of course totally unexpected; 1965 began as a year of promise – the year when the new university department of child health was to be completed at Yorkhill – and nobody could have foreseen that it would end with the original buildings being condemned to destruction.

The first symptoms did not hint at a fatal condition. Investigations, however, continued; consultants were called in; and their diagnosis was grave. J. J. Burnet's building had reached the end of its days. Faults were found in the steel-and-concrete structure; the building was declared to be in a state of 'potential avalanche;' and it was decreed that since continued occupation would be too dangerous the hospital must be evacuated within three months.

The question of where to go, how to get there without a break in emergency work (since there was no other children's hospital in the west of Scotland to take over this duty), and how to achieve this within 12 weeks had now to be faced. In view of the urgency, the board of management decided to delegate their powers to a small *ad hoc* committee charged with carrying out the task. A committee of seven was formed, with Professor Arneil as chairman and Mr Methven as secretary. The group medical superintendent, Dr Park, the matron, Miss Hulme, Mr R. Dunlop, and two surgeons, Mr J. Bentley and Mr D. Macpherson, were the other members of the committee, which contained no board members.

The Western District Hospital, Oakbank – situated off Possil

Road – was chosen by the Western Regional Hospital Board as the hospital's new home. Opened in 1904, Oakbank is a redbrick building of breathtaking grimness, standing near the banks of the derelict Forth and Clyde Canal with not an oak tree in sight. For its new occupants, however, Oakbank posed more than just aesthetic problems – as the *ad hoc* committee soon discovered when they reviewed its structure and dispositions. For a start, there was room for fewer than 200 beds – and Yorkhill had about 300. There was

Oakbank Hospital

no room for the main bio-chemistry department, or for pathology, haematology, medical records, medical illustration, and out-patients. Oakbank had no nurses' teaching department, milk kitchen, or adequate diet kitchen. The staff dining room was too small. A second operating theatre and X-ray room were needed – also a university teaching department and a library, and a much larger casualty department. Patients moving from certain wards to the operating theatres, and from any ward to the X-ray department, would, it was realised, have to travel out of doors on specially built covered trolleys through a narrow courtyard. Throughout the hospital more than 100 windows would have to be made child-proof, hundreds of radiators fitted with guards, all hot pipes covered, all stairs gated – and all banisters made slide-proof.

Altogether 34 building operations, to supply these and other wants, were required. Only 10 weeks remained for the additions and alterations to be planned, constructed, furnished, equipped, and tested; and in addition piped oxygen had to be laid on. In these circumstances much red tape had to be ignored in the to-ings and fro-ings

Goodbye to Yorkhill. The flitting to Oakbank in progress in January 1966.

among the committee, the architects, the contractors, the board of management, and the regional board. By upgrading 20 beds at Drumchapel to accommodate more acute cases the shortage of ward space was made less serious.

Work began. A milk kitchen materialised in what had once been a side ward; a large ground floor ward was turned into a casualty department; the ante-natal clinic was converted into a small lecture theatre – and the dressing cubicles became reading desks.

'It was a period of extreme tension, hustle, and bustle,' recalls one of the committee. At a meeting in a ground-floor ward chalk marks were made on the floor to delineate a future operating theatre suite.

The end of the old Yorkhill.

Stooping to draw a cross on the floor, the chairman of the committee declared: 'This is where we must take the appendix out of an acutely ill child 10 weeks from now.' Some of the contractors' men had once been patients in the children's hospital, and some of their own children were patients at the time. 'They worked day and night,' recalls the committee member. 'The ward floor was dug up and a new floor was laid; the cross remained. Antistatic covering was added and the cross remained. Ten weeks from the first chalk marks an appendix was indeed removed from an acutely ill child at the spot marked by the cross.'

Improvisation was sometimes necessary. Instrument cupboards for one theatre could not be obtained, and so one of the two surgeons on the committee was sent to Lewis's in Argyle Street to buy kitchen units. These served the operating theatre very well for the next six years.

Less than a week before the flitting from Yorkhill was due to begin, a sudden crisis arose; on December 30 it became clear that the old electrical supply cable could not stand the strain of the upgraded hospital. Since power by January 2 was essential, appeals were made to the contractor – and volunteers worked through the New Year period. 'As the men left,' recalls a committee member, 'the medical staff gave each one a bottle of whisky – watched by a weary strayed swan from the canal and a kilted hospital administrator.'

The flitting took place on January 5 and 6, 1966. The committee, who had met crisis after crisis in the final week of preparations, had made plans for every possible contingency – power failures, oxygen troubles, children who were too ill to be moved, and blizzards and other assorted acts of God. In the event the migration was 'an anti-climax of smooth efficiency'. With one operating theatre already dismantled and the equipment transferred to Oakbank, one medical, one surgical, and one orthopaedic unit moved to Oakbank on January 5; and on the following day the second medical and surgical units were transferred, along with the second operating theatre.

During the week before the flitting out-patient work had stopped to allow the casualty work to be done in that department and the casualty department to be moved to Oakbank. When the first patients were transferred at 9 a.m. on January 5, ambulances were diverted and emergency receiving began at Oakbank. 'It should not be forgotten,' remarks one physician, 'that despite the precipitous evacuation the hospital could say of its emergency services, "We never closed." '

In 10 weeks, with the committee working almost round the clock, and with the hospital's and contractor's staff alike exerting all their energies, the busiest children's hospital in Britain had been transferred from a 300-bedded hospital to an old 190-bedded hospital in need of 34 building alterations – a task which had at the outset seemed practically impossible.

So swift and sudden was the transformation of Oakbank that it is not surprising that some of its former patients were taken by surprise. As a small general and maternity hospital Oakbank had been looked upon by people in the neighbourhood as a place where they could always go for help – and expectant mothers had often turned up at the last moment at the obstetrics unit without booking. Some of them continued to do so – and a couple of babies were born in the casualty department.

Chapter 24

YORKHILL REGAINED

In abandoning J. J. Burnet's building the hospital staff were conscious of the cruel irony of leaving behind them at Yorkhill a new block containing an X-ray department and four modern theatres, not to mention the partly built accident and emergency department, university department of child health, and nurses' training school.

'But the dust of demolition work soon settled,' reports Dr Park, the group medical superintendent, 'and while the staff made the greatest possible use of Oakbank, plans were completed to restore the city's paediatric services in a modern building and in the shortest possible time.'

The architects of the new Yorkhill were Baxter Clark and Paul, and Burnet Bell and Partners. Sections of the new building were occupied as they became ready, in advance of the removal of the wards back to Yorkhill. The first buildings to be completed and occupied were those in Yorkhill Court, the staff residential quarters built on former Corporation playing fields. The nurses have occupied their new quarters there for more than three years, travelling to Oakbank by buses provided by the board of management.

The next major instalment, formally handed over in March, 1970, was the laboratory block, housing biochemistry, haematology, and medical genetics. In the same month the first out-patient clinics were held in the new building – in a large, light, and bright department with 27 consulting rooms and five waiting areas. Here, small groups of children and mothers await their turn, their respective wants supplied by rocking horses and comfortable chairs; and the relaxed atmosphere contrasts pleasantly with that of the single

The topping-out ceremony of the new Yorkhill. On the left are Miss Olive Hulme, matron, and Dr Hugh Park, group medical superintendent.

Mr Richard Barclay, chairman of the board, unveils the foundation stone of the new hospital. The stone was the gift of the chief contractors, Richard Costain (Construction) Ltd.

waiting area of the old department, where 'anxious mothers tried vainly to cope with sometimes irritable and frequently bored children.'

Associated with these out-patient clinics are the appliance department and the department of physiotherapy and hydrotherapy. The appliance department work in a large, well-equipped suite, consisting of a metal workshop, leather workshop, and plaster room; and the physiotherapists have at their disposal a large gymnasium, physiotherapy pool, and treatment cubicles.

Out-patient work in the department of child and family psychiatry – housed above the out-patient department – also begun before the occupation of the new wards. The department has also an in-patient section of 20 beds, which came into use at the same time as the general wards. Above the department is a roof-top play area – shades of the old playground on the roof of the Carlile Ward at Garnethill.

The new hospital has an eight-storeyed ward stack. The ground floor consists of administrative offices and stores. On the first floor are the kitchens, which include a butcher's 'shop' and a conveyor belt bearing trays of food selected from the menu by the patients.

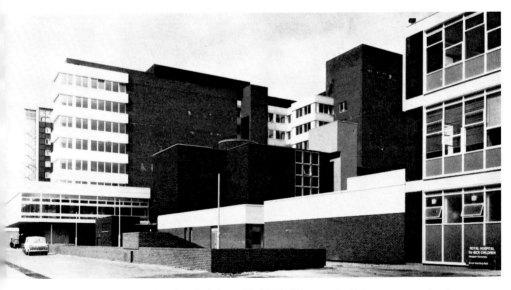

The Royal Hospital for Sick Children, Yorkhill. The new building was completed in 1971.

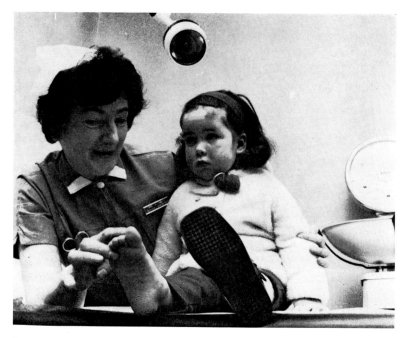

One of the first patients in the new out-patient department, opened in March 1971.

Six ward floors rise above this level. On each floor there are two 24-bedded wards, two tutorial rooms, various offices, a sitting room for mothers who are living in with their children, and an overnight room for far-travelled parents.

One-third of the beds are in single rooms 'for isolation, privacy, or to accommodate a parent with the child'. The wards are allocated to medical paediatrics; surgical paediatrics; ear, nose, and throat surgery; ophthalmology; and dermatology. In addition, one ward is devoted to neonatal surgery and there is a combined medical and surgical ward for cardio-respiratory cases. The new hospital also has an intensive therapy unit, an out-patient theatre, and a cardiology department. Near the university department of child health there is an eight-bed special investigation and treatment unit for multi-disciplinary research programmes.

The cost of building the new Yorkhill was about £5,000,000. The task of equipping and furnishing the new hospital, at a cost of £700,000, of organising the clinical and administrative services (many of which were new to the hospital), and of organising the move

190

back to Yorkhill, fell once again to a commissioning team of six. They were Professor Arneil (convener), Mr Dunlop, Dr Park, Miss Hulme, Mr Macpherson, and Mr Bentley. In the course of two years this team met 170 times for an average of four hours on each occasion.

The task of equipping and furnishing the building was beset by many difficulties and by delays in delivery; and the building itself was not completed by January 1971 as planned. Finally it was handed over on 12 October 1971, and on that day and the next the patients were moved from Oakbank into the first new hospital for children built in Britain for 40 years. Once again, the move was preceded by weeks of frantic preparation; and, once again, the actual transfer went like clockwork. In 48 hours Oakbank was totally emptied, and Yorkhill was regained – six years (almost to the day) after the decision to move to Oakbank was taken.

When the doors of Garnethill were locked for the last time in 1914, 'not a few felt a certain regret'. There were few sorrowful backward glances at the redbrick of Oakbank when, for the second time in its

One of the waiting areas in the new out-patient department.

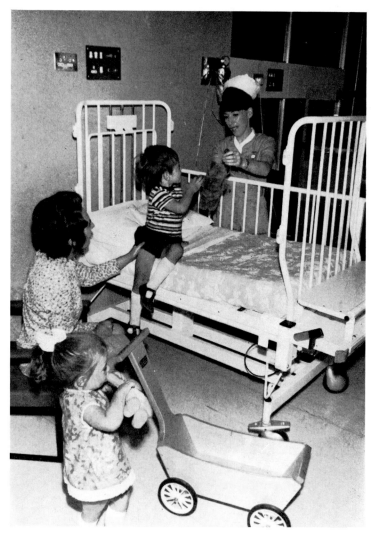

Cheerful scene in one of the wards of the new hospital.

history, the hospital removed itself bodily to Yorkhill. But then, as in 1914, the hospital moved into a modern, well-equipped building designed to put it in the forefront of paediatrics; and then, as before, hopes were high for the future.

In other ways, too, Yorkhill history is curiously repeating itself. When Robert Barclay played his part in the famous opening ceremony on that brilliant July afternoon in 1914, he was not to know that his small son, Richard Barclay – kept at home on that occasion and appeased with banana sandwiches – would play a similar rôle more than half a century later at the inaugural royal visit to a second Yorkhill. Nor can Sir Robert Bruce, who so long ago described the hospital as 'a children's fairy palace on a hill', have guessed that his words would be unknowingly echoed in 1971 by the Russian visitor who described the new hospital as 'a palace of a building that provides the ideal in hospital standards'.

But Robert Barclay and his colleagues, and Andrew Macgeorge and his men before them, have played their part in creating the hospital as it is today. Although the immediate credit goes to the planners, designers, and builders of the new hospital, the achievement is also in a sense part of a much larger endeavour. Whatever dramas of paediatric progress may take place in the new hospital, it should never be forgotten that the Yorkhill story began with an ordinary dwelling house in Garnethill – and with a few men who had faith enough to fight for 20 years to establish a children's hospital in Glasgow.

Appendix

CONSULTANTS AT THE ROYAL HOSPITAL
FOR SICK CHILDREN AT THE TIME OF THE
MOVE BACK TO YORKHILL FROM
OAKBANK, 15TH OCTOBER 1971

Medical Paediatrics
Professor G. C. Arneil
Dr E. N. Coleman
Dr N. A. Coutts
Dr J. O. Craig
Dr W. B. Doig
Dr I. C. Ferguson
Dr W. Hamilton
Professor J. H. Hutchison
Dr J. A. Inall
Dr M. M. Kerr
Dr J. C. Maclaurin
Dr R. A. Shanks
Dr A. L. Speirs
Dr J. B. P. Stephenson
Dr D. H. Wallace

Dermatology
Dr R. L. Cormie
Dr W. N. Morley

Surgical Paediatrics
Mr J. Aitken
Mr J. F. R. Bentley
Mr S. L. Davidson
Mr W. M. Dennison
Mr J. C. Grant
Mr S. L. Mann
Mr. D. G. Young

Orthopaedics
Mr N. J. Blockey
Mr A. N. Conner
Mr D. A. Macpherson
Mr M. G. H. Smith

Ear, Nose and Throat
Dr W. C. Brown
Dr C. E. Gabriel

Cardio-Thoracic Surgery
Mr R. S. Barclay
Mr N. McSwan
Dr J. M. Reid
Dr J. G. Stevenson
Mr T. M. Welsh

Ophthalmology
Dr J. Stanley Cant

Orthodontics
Mr J. A. Russell

Urology
Mr A. G. Graham

Plastic Surgery
Mr J. C. Mustardé

Child and Family Psychiatry
Dr D. S. James
Dr E. C. Nelson
Dr F. H. Stone
Dr I. F. Sutherland

Anaesthetics
Dr W. Auld
Dr C. S. Cairns
Dr H. Fairlie
Dr G. G. France
Dr J. R. Munro
Dr J. B. Stirling

Radiology
Dr M. M. McNair
Dr S. P. Rawson
Dr E. M. Sweet

LABORATORIES

Bacteriology
Dr T. A. McAllister

Biochemistry
Dr R. W. Logan

Haematology
Dr M. L. N. Willoughby

Medical Genetics
Dr M. A. Ferguson-Smith

Pathology
Dr A. A. M. Gibson
Dr A. M. MacDonald

Bibliography

MINUTE BOOK OF THE PROMOTERS OF A CHILDREN'S HOSPITAL IN GLASGOW, 1861–1882 (unpublished)

MINUTE BOOKS OF THE BOARD OF DIRECTORS OF R.H.S.C. (unpublished)

ANNUAL REPORTS OF R.H.S.C., 1883–1947

FINLAYSON, JAMES, Correspondence and Notes on the Extension Proposals to the Royal Hospital for Sick Children, Glasgow, 1885–1906 (unpublished; library of the Royal College of Physicians and Surgeons of Glasgow)

SCRAPBOOK OF GLASGOW UNIVERSITY RELATING TO THE MOVE FROM THE OLD COLLEGE TO GILMOREHILL (unpublished; Glasgow University)

Glasgow Medical Journal – The Bailie – The Bulletin – The Glasgow Herald – The North British Daily Mail – The Regional Review (Journal of the Western Regional Hospital Board, Glasgow)

ARNEIL, GAVIN C., 'Dietary Surveys of Scottish Children in Relation to Rickets' (*Health Bulletin*, vol. XXVI, January 1968)

BOWMAN, A. K., *The Life and Teaching of Sir William Macewen* (London, Edinburgh, and Glasgow, 1942)

BRIDIE, JAMES, *One Way of Living* (London, 1939)

BROTHERSTON, J. H. F., *Observations on the Early Public Health Movement in Scotland.* London School of Hygiene and Tropical Medicine, Memoir No. 8 (London, 1952)

CAMERON, H. C., *The British Paediatric Association, 1928–1952* (London, 1955)

COMRIE, JOHN D., *History of Scottish Medicine*, vol. 2 (London, 1932)

COWAN, JOHN M., *Some Yesterdays* (Glasgow, 1949)

CRAIG, W. S., *Child and Adolescent Life in Health and Disease: A Study in Social Paediatrics* (Edinburgh, 1946)

GLASGOW UNIVERSITY PUBLICATIONS, *The Curious Diversity. Glasgow University on Gilmorehill: the First Hundred Years* (Glasgow, 1970)

NEALE, VICTOR, *The British Paediatric Association, 1952–1968* (London, 1970)

CRAIG, W. S., *John Thomson: Pioneer and Fathers of Scottish Paediatrics* (Edinburgh and London, 1968)

DENNISON, WALLACE M., 'Advances in Paediatric Surgery' (*The Practitioner*, vol. 201, October 1968)

DOWNIE, WALKER, *The Early Physicians and Surgeons of the Western Infirmary* (Glasgow, 1923)

DOWNIE, WALKER, *The Medico-Chirurgical Society of Glasgow, 1814–1907* (Glasgow, 1908)

FERGUSON, THOMAS, *Scottish Social Welfare, 1864–1914* (Edinburgh, 1958)

GIBSON, GEORGE ALEXANDER, *Life of Sir William Tennant Gairdner* (Glasgow, 1912)

FERGUS, JOHN, 'The Medical Institutions of Glasgow' in *The Book of Glasgow* (Glasgow, 1922)

GODLEE, RICKMAN JOHN, *Lord Lister* (Oxford, 1924)

196

GRAHAM, STANLEY, 'Leonard Findlay (1878–1947)' in *Pediatric Profiles* (St Louis, 1957)

GUTHRIE, DOUGLAS, *The Royal Edinburgh Hospital for Sick Children, 1860–1960* (Edinburgh and London, 1960)

HUTCHISON, JAMES H., 'A Century of Paediatrics', *The Practitioner*, July 1968, vol. 201

MACGEORGE, ANDREW, *The Royal Hospital for Sick Children, Glasgow* (Glasgow, 1889)

MACGREGOR, SIR ALEXANDER, *Public Health in Glasgow* (Edinburgh and London, 1967)

MURRAY, IAN, *The Victoria Infirmary of Glasgow: History of a Voluntary Hospital, 1890–1948* (Glasgow, 1967)

NICOLL, JAMES H., 'The Surgery of Infancy', *British Medical Journal*, 18th September, 1909

ORR, JOHN BOYD, *As I Recall* (London, 1966)

PATRICK, JOHN, *A Short History of Glasgow Royal Infirmary* (Glasgow, 1940)

RUSSELL, JAMES BURN, *Public Health Administration in Glasgow* (Glasgow, 1905)

WATERHOUSE, RACHEL, *Children in Hospital: A Hundred Years of Child Care in Birmingham* (London, 1962)

Index

Aberdeen University, 26, 76, 120, 173
Academy of Music, 86
Acidosis and Alkalosis (Graham and Morris), 133
Addenbrooke's Hospital, Cambridge, 84
Aitken, Charles K., 78, 79, 92, 98, 123–4
Alexandra, Queen, 128; Rose Day, 128
All-India Institute of Hygiene and Public Health, 164
Allan Glen's School, 110
American Academy of Paediatrics, 171
American Civil War, 12, 19
Anderson College of Medicine, 59, 61, 78, 120
Anderson, Dr A. D., 18
Anderson, David, 24, 25, 28
Anderson, J. B. MacKenzie, 63, 77, 78
Anderston Weavers' Society, 47
Arneil, Professor Gavin, 156, 162, 164, 169, 170, 173–4, 181, 191
Asylum for the Blind, 48
Athenaeum Gymnastic Club, 47

Bailie, The, 11, 21, 35, 43, 44, 50, 51, 54
Baird, Professor Dugald, 120
Baird, John, and James Thomson, 53
Baird Smith, Barclay and Muirhead, 151
Balfour of Burleigh, Lord, 48
Bamber, Sister, 136–7
Band of Hope (Cambuslang), 48
Bannerman, Charlotte, 139
Barclay lectureship, 116, 118, 119, 125, 161, 179
Barclay Mr Richard H., 149, 150, 151, 188, 193
Barclay, Robert F., 79, 89, 92, 101, 106, 123–4, 127, 130, 136, 138, 146, 149, 151, 192–3
Barony Church, 10, 26
Baxter Clark and Paul, 187
Bellahouston gold medal, 156
Bentley, Mr John, 159, 181, 191
Bilsland, Sir William, 82
Bird, Robert, 82
Birmingham, 16, 102, 147

Blacklock, John W. S., 116, 130, 131, 133
Blockey, Mr Noel, 161, 163, 179
Blythswood, Lord, 83
Boer War, 62, 72
Bothwell Park brickworks, 89
Bowman, Dr A. K., 35, 37, 111
Boyd, J. Glen, 127
Breadalbane, Marquis and Marchioness of, 48
Bridie, James, *see* Mavor, O. H.
British Architect, The, 55
British Broadcasting Company, 106
British Hospitals Association, 125
British Medical Association, 45, 102
British Order of Ancient Free Gardeners, 49
British Paediatric Association, 155, 171
Bruce, Sir Robert, 127, 193
Brussels Conservatory, 121
Buccleuch Street, 24, 28, 43, 80
Buchanan, Sir George Leith, 51
Bulletin, The, 104
Burdett, Henry C., 52
Burnett Bell and Partners, 187
Burnet, John, and Son, 53
Burnet, John (senior), 86
Burnet, John James, 54, 84, 86, 87, 88, 89, 122, 181, 187

Caird, Principal, 26
Cairns, Dr R. O., 153
Caldecott, Randolph, illustrations, 28
Cambridge University, 114
Cameron, Dr Agnes, 120
Cameron, D. Y., 62
Cameron, Sir Hector, 35–6, 70, 71, 74, 75, 81, 82, 83, 95, 111
Cameron, Hector Charles, 36, 111
Cameron, Miss Mary, 137–8
Campbell Douglas and Sellars 53
Carlile, Thomas, 43–4, 78
Carlile ward, 66, 94, 189
Carmen (chimpanzee), 173–4
Cathcart, Professor Edward P., 126
Central Station 'Shell', 129

Chadwick, Edwin, 12, 16
Christian, Princess, 65
Church of Scotland, 20
Chalmers, Dr A. K., 71
Charles, Sister Edith, 145
Children's Clinical Club, 72–3
Children's Home Hospital, Strathblane, 148, 151
Children's Research Fund, 167
Children's Tinfoil League, 128
Chris, Sister, 67
City Chambers, 82
Clapperton, Alan E., 79, 125–6, 127
Clarkson, R. D., 177
Clarkson, Miss Ruth, 175–7
Clinical Hospital and Dispensary for Children, Manchester, 38
Clyde, River, 12, 84, 144
Clydesdale Bank, 86
Coachmen of Glasgow, 47
Coats, Joseph, 40
Coats, Peter, 108
Coleman, Dr Eric, 162
Committee of Glasgow Coachmen Grooms and Friends, 47
Costain, Richard (Construction), Ltd, 188
Cot:
    Amateur Dramatic Club, 49
    Carrick Buchanan, 49
    Glasgow Students' Charities Day, 129
    Magpie Minstrels, 49
    People's Friend Cot, The, 49
    Philomel, 49
    Sister Elizabeth, 49
    Weekly Herald, The, Guild of Kindness, 49
    West of Scotland, 49
Country branch, see Drumchapel
Cowan and Fraser, 78
Cowan, Clapperton, and Barclay, 79
Cowan, Fraser, and Clapperton, 78–9
Cowan, James, 88–9
Cowan, Dr John B., 10–11, 15, 17
Cowan, John M., 62
Cowcaddens, 12, 16, 53, 59, 64, 81, 164
Crimea, 10, 31, 94
Cystic Fibrosis Research Foundation, 167

Daily Record, The, 102
Dalziel, T. Kennedy, 67–8, 70, 74–5, 80, 81, 82, 83, 93, 99
Davidson, Mr Sam, 158, 159
Dennison, Wallace, 119, 133, 158, 159, 161, 171
Dennistoun Amateur Minstrels, 47

Department of Health for Scotland, 138, 145, 171
Dods, Rev. Marcus, 26
Dollan, Lord Provost 'Paddy', 145
Downie, J. Walker, 39
Drumchapel, 66–7, 108, 145, 148, 179, 183
Drumchapel Hospital for geriatric patients, 148, 164
Drummond, Rev. Dr Henry, 26
Duke Street Prison, Governor of, 90
'Duke, the', see Macleod, Dr George H. B.
Dunlop, Mr Robert, 152, 153, 191
Dunlop, Sir Thomas, 149–51

East Park Home, 162
Edinburgh, 10, 11, 12, 81
Edinburgh University, 74, 171
Elgin Place Literary and Home Reading Circle, 47
Elinor, Sister, 169
Elizabeth, Princess, 128
Elliot, Walter, 119
Elmbank Stravaigers, 47
Endowments Commission, 149
European Society for Paediatric Nephrology, 171
Evening Citizen, The, 91
Ewing, Archibald Orr, M.P., 9, 54–5,

Faculty of Physicians and Surgeons of Glasgow, 39
'Fancy Fair' (1884), 50–1, 53
Fergus, Dr Freeland, 39–40
Ferguson-Smith, Dr Malcolm, 167
Findlay, Leonard, 110–13, 114, 115, 120, 121, 124, 154, 162, 167, 169, 171, 177
Fine Arts Institute, 48, 151
Finlayson, James, 35, 37–40, 42–3, 44, 46, 67, 72–3, 74, 77, 83
First World War, 41, 49, 59, 61, 72, 74, 77, 112, 115, 116, 120, 121, 129, 133, 146
Fleming, Geoffrey B., 114–15, 131, 146, 154, 156
Fleming, J. P. ('Pim'), 120
Fleming, John Gibson, 18
Ford, Dr Findlay, 149, 171
Forth and Clyde Canal, 182
Fraser Foundation, 162
Fraser, (Sir) Matthew P., 79
Free Church of Scotland, 20
From Glasgow's Treasure Chest, 88–9

Gairdner, William T., 15, 23, 55, 57
Galloway, H. H., 79
Gamp, Sarah, 31
Gardiner research lectureship, 101, 130, 149, 162, 171
Garnethill, 24 28–33, 34, 65, 67, 71, 73, 74, 75, 77, 78, 79, 80, 81, 85, 87, 88, 89, 97, 101, 110, 119, 125, 128, 130, 133, 134, 157, 173, 189, 191, 193
Garnethill Convent School, 94
Gemmell, Samson, 40, 74, 76, 77, 110; Chair of Medical Paediatrics (now the Chair of Child Health), 40 101, 102, 110, 114, 119, 134, 154, 156, 167, 171
General Nursing Council, 136
George V, King, 91, 102, 104
Gibbon, Lewis Grassic, 142
Gilbert, Andrew, 84–5
Gilbert, C. A. Crerar, 85
Gilbert, Mrs Crerar, 85
Gilmorehill, 22, 23, 144, 172
Glasgow:
    Academy, 60, 77, 78
    and District Children's Hospitals, 148
    and West of Scotland Association for the Return of Women to Local Boards, 66
    Art Gallery, 26, 85, 102
    Charity Organisation Society, 57
    Corporation, 15, 30, 86, 98, 123, 164, 167, 170
    Education Department, 123
    High School, 38, 116, 125
    Royal Infirmary, 10, 17, 18–19, 22, 31, 33, 35, 37, 38, 45, 62, 76, 77, 78, 91
    Stock Exchange, Association, 124
    Student's Charities Day, 128–9
    University, 10, 20, 22, 23, 26, 36, 40, 60, 62, 77, 78, 80, 82, 84, 99, 101, 110, 116, 119, 120, 125, 126, 130, 134, 156, 160, 164, 171, 173
    Western Infirmary, 10, 17, 22, 23, 33, 36, 38, 39, 45, 59, 61, 74, 75, 77, 84, 86, 110, 137, 154
Glasgow Herald, The, 18, 24, 50, 74, 91, 105, 106, 108, 127
Glasgow Medical Journal, The, 10
Glasgow News, The, 82, 90
Goodrich, Rev. Albert, 26
Gourlay, Mrs R. Cleland, 128
Govan Rob Roy Four-in-Hand Club, 47
Gow, Leonard, 101
Gow lecturership, 110, 114, 154, 156

Gracie, Captain, 96
Graham, Mrs Stanley, 156
Graham, Professor Stanley, 110, 111, 112, 113, 115, 119, 131, 133, 149, 154, 155–6, 171, 175
Graham-Gilbert, John, 85
Grand Theatre, 58
Great Ormond Street Hospital, London, 11, 32, 87, 161, 177
Great Plague, 13
Greenlees, James, 120
Guthrie, Dr Katherine, 157

Hamilton, Dr William, 162
Hampden Park, 47
Harbin, Mrs Louisa, 32, 43, 59, 90, 122, 134, 175, 177, 180
Hengler's Circus, 48
Honeyman, Keppie, and Mackintosh, 86
Hospital for Women, Leeds, 138
Howard and Wyndham, 58
Hulme, Miss Olive, 175–7, 179, 180, 181, 188, 191
Hutchieson, Harry, 120
Hutchison, Professor James, 99, 101, 113, 119, 131, 133, 154, 155, 156, 157, 164, 166, 167, 169, 170–1, 173
Hyndland Church, 28

Illingworth, Sir Charles, 126
Industrial Revolution, 12
International Collaborative Study of Kidney Disease in Children, 169
Invernairn, Lord, 129

Jordanhill Training College, 131

Kay, Professor Andrew, 120
Kelvin Hall, 102, 173, 174
Kelvin, Lord, 82, 85
Kelvin, River, 22

Lafferty, Helen ('Princess Helen'), 102
Laird, Mr Andrew P., 144, 158, 159, 171, 173
Lang, Dr Marshall, 26
Laura, Sister, 58–9, 64, 136
Lazarus, Master Solomon, 90
League of Nations Red Cross Society, Geneva, 112
Leicester Infirmary, 32

Leishman, William, 35, 40
Lenihan, Dr J. M. A., 64, 170
Lennox Hospital, 145
Lipton, Sir Thomas, 82
Lister, Lord, 10, 35
Little Brick Builders, The, 82–3
Loch Katrine, 13
Lochhead, Alfred, 86, 90
Logan, Dr Robert, 162
London College of Medicine, 63
London Zenana Medical College, 65
Louise, Princess, 65
Lowe, Maister Peter, 39

McAllister, Dr Anne, 131
MacAllister, Sir Donald, 80, 84, 101, 102, 105
McArthur, Dr Patrick, 171
MacDonald, Dr Alistair, 162
Macewen, William, 35–6, 37, 59, 74, 76
Macfarlane, Douglas, 120
Macgeorge, Andrew, 20–1, 23, 24, 29, 31, 55, 57, 78, 125, 151, 193
Macgeorge, Cowan, and Fraser, 78
McKendrick, Professor, 51
Mackenzie, Agnes Mure, 16
Mackintosh, Charles Rennie, 86
Mackintosh, Dr Donald J., 84, 86, 87
McLaren, Dr Alice, 62–3, 66, 120
Maclay, Murray and Spens, 151
MacLellan, Mrs Alexander, 149, 150, 151, 179, 180
MacLennan, Alexander, 116–18, 119, 129, 133, 134, 138, 159, 161
Macleod, Dr (later Sir) George H. B., 10, 11, 17, 49, 57
Macleod, Rev. Dr Norman, 10, 17, 26
Macnaughton, Mr, 48
McNeil, Dr C. Kerr, 160
Macpherson, Mr Duncan, 161, 181, 191
MacPherson, Ian, 120
Macrae, Farquhar, 62
Mann, Mr Stewart, 159, 173
Mary, Princess, 92, 102, 104
Mary, Queen, 91, 102, 104
Mavor, O. H., 77, 78, 119, 120
Maylard, A. E., 76
Mearnskirk Hospital, 145, 162
Medical Research Council, 157, 166, 168
Medico-Chirurgical Society of Glasgow, 18
Merchants' House, 16, 123, 151
Methven, James, 127, 152, 153, 181
Middleton, George, 76–7, 82

Ministry of Health, 148
Miss Cranston's tearoom, 128
Montgomery, Dr George, 149, 162, (Professor) 171
Montrose, Duchess of, 50
Montrose, Duke of, 55, 91
Morris, Noah, 115–16, 130, 131, 133, 164
Mr Vallance's Elocution Pupils' Entertainment, 47
Muir, (Sir) Robert, 40, 113
Muirhead, Miss Sophia, 131, 161
Muller, Professor Max, 47
Murray, Surgeon Captain, 63

National Health Act, 148, 149
National Health Service, 46, 127, 167, 168, 177
Neilson, Sister Isabel, 137
Ness, Barclay, 41, 63, 72, 77–8, 119, 123
Nicoll, James, 37, 59–62, 64, 77, 83, 99, 124, 134, 159, 161, 173
Nightingale, Florence, 31, 94, (of Yorkhill) 137
North and South Ayrshire Hospitals, 153
North British Daily Mail, 19, 24
Northern Regional Hospital Board, 171
Nuffield, Lord, 128
Nursing and Midwives' Journal, 89

Oakbank Hospital, 153, 177, 179, 181–6, 187
Old College, 22
Orpheus Club, 47
Orr, Lord John Boyd, 40, 72, 147
Orr, Dr Robert Scott, 18

Park, Dr Hugh, 152, 153, 165, 181, 187, 188, 191
Parliamentary Commission on Hospitals, 106
Parry, Robert H., 41, 74, 75–6, 80, 119
Paterson, Mrs Margaret Montgomery, 66
Paton, Professor Diarmid Noel, 112
People's Friend, The, 49, 58
People's Fund, The, 82
Phaire, Thomas, *The Boke of Chyldren*, 34
Philomel Club, 47
Poor Laws, Commissioner of the, 12
Practical Paediatric Problems (Professor James Hutchison), 156
Price, Rees, 64

Pringle, J. Hogarth, 62
Public Health (Scotland) Act, 13

Queen:
Alexandra, 128; Rose Day, 128
Elizabeth Hospital for Children, London, 113
Margaret College, 65, 120
Mother's Hospital, 91, 148, 157, 159, 167
Victoria, 65; Diamond Jubilee, 65
Queen's Rooms, 47

Rait, Robert, Principal of Glasgow University, 82
Ramstedt's operation, 134
Rankin, William, 116, 119, 120, 125
Raphael's Sistine Madonna, 123, 149
Rawson, Dr Simon, 162, 174
Red Cross, 146
Redlands Hospital for Women, 63
Regional Department of Clinical Physics and Bio-engineering, 170
Reid, Miss Anna, 128
Religious Institution Rooms, 9, 11
Richards, Dr Gerald, 167
Robertson, Miss Hannah, 153
Robinson, Miss (of London), 32
Robinson, Miss Olivia, 117, 137, 138, 144, 145, 177
Röntgen Ray apparatus, 63
Royal and Ancient Golf Club, 124
Royal:
Clyde Yacht Club, 151
College of Physicians and Surgeons of Glasgow, 171
College of Physicians of London, 171
Faculty of Physicians and Surgeons of Glasgow, 78, 123
Hospital for Sick Children, Edinburgh, 120, 177
Maternity Hospital, 101
Princess Theatre, 47
Russell, Dr James B., 32, 68–9, 71
Scots Greys, 92
Scottish Automobile Club, 130

St Andrew's Hall, 25, 50, 51
St Andrews University, 36
Samaritan Hospital, 63
Scott Street, 24, 63, 65, 75, 90, 93, 94
Scottish:
Association of Paediatric Surgeons, 171

Football Association, 47
Hospitals Endowments Research Trust, 167
National Academy of Music, 126
Paediatric Society, 120
Zoo, 47
Second World War, 76, 108, 118, 119, 121, 122, 133, 143, 144, 166
Secretary of State for Scotland, 149, 167
Sedate Club, 47
Seligmann, Sigismund, 48
Sellars, James, 25, 30, 53, 54, 87
Shanks, Dr Robert, 162, 163, 173
Siam, Prince and Princess of, 102
Simpson, Miss Julia, 90, 93, 97, 137, 173
Skating Palace, 47
Smith, David, 17
Smith, Laura M., see Laura, Sister
Society for the Study of Children's Diseases, 72
Standing Medical Advisory Committee, 171
Steven, John Lindsay, 62
Stevenson, Dr Mary, 110, 121
Stewart, Charles E., 82
Stobhill Hospital, 95, 116
Stocquart, Dr Elaine, 121
Stone, Dr Frederick, 165
Strong, Mrs Rebecca, 31
Sunderland Children's Infirmary, 137
Sussex (cruiser), 144
Suttie, David Campbell, 121–2, 125, 137, 144–5, 153, 162, 165

Templeton and Co., James, 134
Templeton, Mr Andrew R., 149
Tharsis Copper and Sulphur Company, 48
Theatre Royal, 47
Thomson, John (of Edinburgh), 73, 101, 111, 113, 177
Toronto University, 154
Townhead Public School, 48
Trades House, 16, 123
Trinity Congregational Church, 39
Turnbull, Sister Jane, 136

Ulster Hospital, Belfast, 138
University Avenue, department of child psychology, 165
Urie, Miss Jane, 139

Victoria Infirmary, 33, 76

Victoria, Queen, 65; Diamond Jubilee, 65

Watson, Miss Margaret, 139–42
Webster, Dr Alfred, 62
West Balgray House, Kelvinside, 84
West Graham Street, 53, 58, 59, 60, 62, 63, 64, 67, 96, 116, 164
Western:
   and Northern Grocers' Soirée Committee 47
   District Hospital, Oakbank, The, *see* Oakbank Hospital
   Isles, 142–3
   Medical Club, 39
   Regional Hospital Board, 64, 111, 148, 181–2
White, Matthew, 95, 116, 118–119, 120, 121, 131, 133, 149, 159, 171
Whitelaw, James T., 24, 25, 29, 43, 55, 87
Willoughby, Dr Michael, 168
Wilson, Dr Ellis, 162–4, 173
Woodlands Terrace, day centre, 165

Workman, Charles, 62

York, Duchess of, 128
Yorkhill Children's and Maternity Hospitals, 148
Yorkhill Court, 180, 187
Yorkhill Hospital:
   architects of, (old) 86, 122; (new) 187
   construction and design of, old, 87–90
   cost of, (old building) 89, (new building) 190
   in wartime, 95–8, 144–7
   incorporated as a company, 123
   migration to Oakbank, 181–6
   old building condemned to destruction, 181
   opening of, (old building) 89, 91–3, 130, 151, 192–3; (new building) 187–193
   site purchased for, old building, 84
Yorkhill House, 84, 85
Young, Alfred, 62, 67
Young, Professor Archibald, 134
Young, Mr Dan, 159, 165
Young, Fred H., 134